RS

Library of Congress Cataloging-in-Publication Data

Steinhoff, Johannes.
    [In letzter Stunde. English]
    The final hours : the Luftwaffe plot against Göring / Johannes Steinhoff ; foreword by Dennis E. Showalter.—1st ed.
        p. cm.—(Aviation classics)
    Originally published in English in 1977 under the title The Last chance.
    Includes index.
    ISBN 1-57488-863-3 (alk. paper)
    1. Steinhoff, Johannes.   2. Germany. Luftwaffe—Biography.   3. World War, 1939–1945—Personal narratives, German.   4. World War, 1939–1945—Aerial operations, German.   5. Fighter pilots—Germany—Biography.   6. World War, 1939–1945—Germany.   7. Göring, Hermann, 1893–1946.   I. Title.   II. Series: Aviation classics series (Washington, D.C.)

D811.S794513 2004
940.54′4943′092—dc22   2004012842

Printed in Canada on acid-free paper that meets the American National Standards Institute Z39-48 Standard.

Potomac Books, Inc.
22841 Quicksilver Drive
Dulles, Virginia 20166

First Edition

10 9 8 7 6 5 4 3 2 1

THE FINAL HOURS

Series Editors

Walter J. Boyne and Peter B. Mersky

Aviation Classics are inspired nonfiction and fictional accounts that reveal the human drama of flight. The series covers every era of military and civil aviation, is international in scope, and encompasses flying in all of its diversity. Some of the books are well-known best-sellers and others are superb, but unheralded, titles that deserve a wider audience.

Other titles in the Aviation Classics series

THE FINAL HOURS
The Luftwaffe Plot Against Göri...

Johannes Steinhoff

Foreword by Dennis E. Showalter

Potomac Books, Inc.
Washington, D.C.

CONTENTS

FOREWORD

I first discovered Johannes Steinhoff as a graduate student, preparing a field in World War II. His name kept appearing as one of the gifted warriors who carried the Third Reich on their shoulders for six years. Never did men fight better in a worse cause than did the Germans from 1939 to 1945, and Steinhoff was a paladin. As a fighter pilot he served on every major front and scored 176 aerial victories. He was among the first to fly jets in combat, serving with the famous "Squadron of Experts" in the war's final days. He had been decorated with the Knight's Cross with Swords and Oak Leaves. While his awards might have been bestowed by a criminal regime, the skill and bravery they recognized were no less real for that. There was also a certain karmic irony in someone often called "the handsomest man in the Luftwaffe" having his face burned off in a crash just at the end of the war, eventually emerging from years of restorative surgery with a gargoyle mask that was mostly scar tissue. It required little imagination to interpret Johannes Steinhoff as a symbol of Germany itself: disfigured by its past, permanently marked for everyone to see. I regularly suggested the trope to my classes, and considered myself a clever young professor indeed.

It required no more research than reading German newspapers to discover that Johannes Steinhoff was more than a symbol of a vanished regime and a lost war. When the newly established Federal Republic of Germany began considering recreating its armed forces as part of its reintegration into an emerging Western Alliance, Steinhoff was among the first veterans consulted. He had won general respect for his integrity, and for his willingness to challenge openly what he considered the disastrously mistaken operational decisions of Hitler and his lieutenant, Luftwaffe commander Hermann Göring. Initially reluctant, like many of his counterparts, to consider putting on a uniform once more, Steinhoff finally decided that he might after all be able to contribute directly to creating a new Germany. It would not be a Germany of power and conquest like its Imperial and National Socialist predecessors. Nor would it be the "Holy Germany," a beacon to the nations, of which resisters like Col. Claus von Stauffenberg had dreamed. This Germany would be a state and a people among others, committed to a common European and Atlantic enterprise. Resisting the ideological and military challenges of the Soviet Union was merely a first step toward the eventual construction of a community of free peoples, linked by mutual interests and mutual respect. He saw German-American relations as the cornerstone of that enterprise.

Johannes Steinhoff became one of the founding fathers of a new Luftwaffe, whose officers and men served a democracy in the context of the NATO Alliance. He eventually rose to be its Inspector-General, then its Chairman of the Military Commission of NATO, retiring as a four-star general. Neither he nor his pilots ever fired a shot in anger. In his later years, Steinhoff described that as the aspect of his career of which he was most proud.

I learned that during our collaboration on a book titled *Voices from the Third Reich*. In 1985 President Ronald Reagan made international headlines by standing alongside German Chancellor Helmut Kohl to commemorate German war dead at Bitburg, in a cemetery including some graves of SS men. General Steinhoff, by then retired, attended the ceremony, and was shaken by the negative reactions it evoked in Europe and the United States. Johannes had told his own wartime story, in *The Straits of Messina* and this volume, *The Final Hours*. But he believed there was a larger story to tell: the story of the German people, especially the generation that had fought World War II in the front lines. After Bitburg it was especially important for him that Americans come to understand the complex web of circumstances and principles that brought Adolf Hitler to power and held Germany in his thrall until nothing remained.

To tell the story, Johannes decided he needed an American collaborator. By then I was teaching at Colorado College. Johannes's son-in-law was also on the faculty, in a different department, and the General and I had met casually a couple of times. When his daughter suggested "What about Dennis?" he was willing to consider it. We met, talked, and came to a quick agreement.

For me it was the start of an adventure. "We'll be working in each others' pockets for a long time," Johannes told me. "I want someone who can discuss more than today's newspaper." It didn't take me long to discover that the general was a man of *Bildung*, of cultivation, in the best sense of that distinctively German concept. He was widely, indeed universally, read, in history, literature, and philosophy. He sympathized with my ignorance of Greek and Latin. He was an accomplished amateur artist. And well into his seventies he could pull Gs in an F-4 Phantom jet. It was not a combination of characteristics usually found in an American senior officer, to say the least!

Wherever we went in Germany as we worked on the project, General Steinhoff was recognized and respected. "My face is hard to forget," he would joke. But it was his personality that made the impression. Whether interviewing veterans and survivors of the war, talking with men who served with him in the Bundeswehr, or acknowledging seekers of an autograph or a handshake in a restaurant, Johannes stood out. He was no shrinking violet. He enjoyed the attention and he knew his worth. But he did not need to seek center stage. The spotlight sought him.

For many of his countrymen, on all points of the political spectrum, Johannes Steinhoff epitomized the "new Germany" of the Federal Republic. Conscious of the past, he had learned from it, without either obsessing on or forgetting his part in it. His memories were never self-protective. "I was part of a generation," he would say, "that was raised on the myths of patriotism and sacrifice. Hitler appealed to those myths, and led us to destruction. Never forget that the German people followed him. But never forget that Hitler's Reich lasted twelve years, while Germany's history spans a thousand." He had no use for the argument that German culture or the German people were somehow inherently flawed. "People can learn, and grow, and change. The challenge is never to stop living, even if at times you lose your way."

Johannes never stopped living and kept looking forward until the day of his death. To call him a great man would be to inspire his laughter. "Heroes and martyrs are always scarce. Love your country and stand for truth. That's the best one can do." But Johannes Steinhoff was a remarkable man. As a young pilot he epitomized courage and honor, at a time when courage was too often betrayed and honor too often mocked. In his later years he stood for Western culture and Atlantic civilization even when both concepts fell out of fashion. Readers of *The Final Hours* will respond in a variety of ways—but never with indifference.

DENNIS E. SHOWALTER, PH.D.

PREFACE

Significant war literature and war memoirs from the point of view of Germany's participation in World War II are scarce indeed. The best of the lot was written by an Alsatian, Guy Sajer's *The Forgotten Soldier*. The rest of the literature falls generally into two categories: generals writing in the genre of "if the *Führer* had only listened to me!" and fighter pilots or tank busters writing about their heroics against the productive flood from America or the primitive masses of the Soviet Union.

Johannes Steinhoff has written a work that stands far above such memoir literature for its integrity and sense of tragedy. Not only that, but it is stunningly well-written and translated. Steinhoff's account then is not about heroic efforts to stem the tide of the Allied air offensive against Germany, but rather reveals an attempt, tragically late— fully recognized as such by the author—to remove *Reichsmarschall* Hermann Göring from his position as commander in chief of the Luftwaffe in the winter of 1944–1945—to remove him for a gross ineptitude that he had in fact been exhibiting from 1940.

The book begins, however, with Steinhoff's riveting account of how in the first months after the war he had had to come to grips with himself and his past. Crashing in an Me 262 in April 1945, Steinhoff was terribly burned and had virtually nothing left of his face. In the months following the war, as German doctors with few medicines available operated again, and again, and again, to put his face back together, Steinhoff faced his past. Unlike the Mansteins, the Guderians, and the Rudels who pretended in their memoirs that they had been only soldiers with no knowledge of "war crimes," Steinhoff remembers what he calls "the disgrace of our nation," Auschwitz,

Treblinka, and Buchenwald. "As if we had not known—but it was unthinkable and we had simply closed our ears to it, there being no alternative in the pursuit of ultimate victory."

Steinhoff's account of the wounded in his burn ward—veterans of different services with but one common experience—the horror of their injuries, is touching, humorous, and above all courageous. His roommate, horribly burned in a Tiger tank in the 1945 battles in Silesia (not all Tigers destroyed thousands of Russian tanks), a lance corporal, faces the same terrible battle. In a sense these burned men with no faces are an allegory for a nation wrecked from one end to the other—its past, discredited and disgraceful—their courage, its hope for the future.

Steinhoff's book then is a book of ironies. The frontline officers did not plot to overthrow a regime that had thrown the German nation over the precipice, but rather to remove the man responsible for the catastrophe in the air war—and to fire him nearly three quarters of a year *after* the Luftwaffe had been irrevocably defeated in the skies over Europe. They clearly hoped that his replacement could bring some improvement to the conduct of the air battle. Such hopes were idle, the war had been lost, and the full horror of that defeat was coming home to a German nation ravaged from the air and wrecked on the ground by advancing Allied armies.

The final sections deal with Steinhoff's last days as a pilot, the last desperate battles against the masses of American bombers and fighters, and the last shattering flight in a Me 262 that led to the hospital. This is then an account well worth reading—an account of an honest man who has faced his past and whose present indicates how far Germany has come since the dark days of 1945.

WILLIAMSON MURRAY, PH.D.

INTRODUCTION

A man who is not a professional author ought not, it seems to me, to write a book unless he feels irresistibly compelled to do so. Why, then, did I *have* to write this book?

In my case the compulsion arose out of *my* profession: I am a soldier and an airman. The force that, with the end of the Second World War already in sight, drove us to conspire against our commander in chief and ultimately demand his resignation was first and foremost a conflict of the soldierly conscience. It had been clear to us for a long time that we were incompetently and irresponsibly commanded. Powerless to alter the fact that we were equipped with unsuitable material, we were obliged to submit to insults and to accusations of cowardice for being unable to turn that material to account in terms of military successes. When it finally dawned on us—far too late: our education had seen to that—that our generation had been ushered into a wanton and criminal war, we were faced squarely with the problem of military insubordination.

The conspiracy of 20 July 1944 had failed. Many of us who were still fighting at the front at that time had at first been shocked by what Count Stauffenberg and his associates had set out to do. We lacked the insight that alone can shape such decisions. Nor had we any means of attaining it; we were much too busy scrambling to think any further ahead than the day in hand. What was expected of us was that we should return victorious from the next mission with kills to our credit. It was what we expected of ourselves. Because we were more than just soldiers: we were fanatical fliers, whose enthusiasm had been systematically kindled and nourished and whose achievements had been consistently rewarded with decorations and privileges. Our desire for achievement was on the one hand natural and spontaneous because we were young and because that was how we had been brought up; on the other hand we had been corrupted without knowing it. Not until we had been pulled back from the outlying fronts onto German soil and become captive witnesses of the destruction of our cities, unable—because we were wrongly equipped and wrongly engaged—to do anything effective about preventing it, did we young Luftwaffe officers grasp in our turn that we had been resoundingly had.

But it was too late; there could not be another 20 July. We knew that. Ours was a conspiracy without hope. For most of us the step to insubordination was quite literally appalling, but we had to take it; subordination had become more than we could bear. Granted, our whole undertaking was a case of "too little, too late"—we still had to go through with it, in order to be able to justify ourselves to ourselves. However corny that may sound today (and it is going to be difficult to convey the sort of state of mind we pilots were in at that time), it is none the less true.

In recalling these events, which had long remained buried in my memory, it has not been my intention to make excuses. Our unconditional self-sacrifice in the service of the Third Reich is too well documented for that; so are our dissipation and debauchery, the boozing with which we stupefied ourselves, the sheer youthful lust for life that spent itself in fornication. Nor has my purpose been merely to supply a hitherto missing piece of Luftwaffe history. Least of all was I moved by a desire to launch yet more "revelations" on the latest wave of literature dealing with the Third Reich.

This book stands in a wider context. It is a contribution to the history of my generation, the surviving members of which were pushed by the war beyond the limits of their physical and mental endurance. And we survivors, who not long after the war set about building a completely different kind of state with the same people as had constituted the old, demand to be understood. It is essential that we be understood, because the value of what we have created since attaining to positions of leadership is by no means uncontested today. When one of the freest countries in the world can exhibit a kind of frustration with, not to say aversion to, that freedom, when large numbers of inexperienced young people can fail to consider that country worth defending, then some of us have got to tell it the way it was. For this reason I am even prepared to welcome the German publishing industry's current Third Reich wave—in so far as it is prompted by a serious desire to throw light on our history and not, as most "waves" are, merely by the lure of profit.

So it is because of what is happening today—with freedom threatened in virtually every respect by its own abuse—that I offer this contribution, in the form of an episode in which I was myself involved, to the history of the soldier in the twentieth century. Soldiers have always, in every century of their existence, been victims of the ruthless misuse of power; indeed, given the opportunity, they have joined in the power game themselves. But it fell to our own century to accomplish, with the aid of a whole technology of mass extermination, the most atrocious massacres in the history of mankind. This fact alone makes pacifism a philosophy worthy of respect, and I have a great deal of sympathy with those who profess it. In the highest positions of military command that it has been my good fortune to have filled I never qualified my whole-hearted agreement with the many politicians who, abhorring war, set themselves no higher goal than to prevent it. It is a poor show and says little for man's supposedly increasing maturity that the prevention of a third world war has not so far succeeded by any other means than by armament, deterrence, and nuclear stalemate. I am not one of those who think they have the answer to the problems and perplexities of the world. I too, occupying a responsible position in the hierarchy of an international defensive alliance, was able to do no more than play a part in maintaining peace by means of armament, deterrence, and nuclear stalemate. Plain common sense knows that such means are, to say the least, agonizingly circuitous. But as long as there exist ideologies whose sense of mission will not permit them to forgo the use of brute military force to achieve their ends, clearly the roundabout way to peace will be the only one.

The figure of the soldier in all his manifestations is thus symptomatic of the century now nearing its close, and it is to the history of that figure that I wish to contribute by describing what happened to me. I have tried to show what it is possible to do to men, how insidiously they can be manipulated by education, how they can be hoisted onto a pedestal as "heroes," how they can be so corrupted as even to enjoy the experience—and how they can be dropped and denounced as mutineers when they discover that they have scruples.

The complete lack of scruples that such treatment implies is peculiar to rulers who believe that the problems of their own and other peoples can be solved by imposing, through the use of military force, peace on their, the rulers', terms—in our case a *pax germanica*, but the second Latin word is readily interchangeable.

All documents and extracts from the minutes of discussions with Göring as well as the extracts from the diary of the Chief of General Staff of the Luftwaffe come from the *Militargeschichliches Forschungasamt* in Freiburg.

PROLOGUE

Oberföhring Army Hospital, Munich
July 1945

We were dumped here three weeks ago after an involuntary pilgrimage through the army hospitals and POW camps of Bavaria. They off-loaded us—the three "facial burns"—from a big American truck in the hope that perhaps somebody here could help us.

So I am back in the hospital where I was treated immediately after my crash. My companions are Chief Executive Officer Karl Recknagel of the Imperial Meteorological Service and Lance-Corporal Alfons Holzamer of the Pan-German Army, last position—i.e., before he got his wound—tank driver. We are seasoned patients. We also—although of widely different origins and occupations—share a common fate that has forged close personal ties: our faces have been destroyed by fire.

Together we are battling through the no-man's-land of medical attention that began for us with the end of the Third Reich. We know all the dodges. We are past masters at the art of survival, of "organizing" things (food, dressings, ointments, sleeping pills—you name it). We have been through Bad Wiessee, Beuerberg, and Allgasing. In Bad Wiessee they helped me beat tetanus, and we stuck together like glue when the Americans entered the hospital. In Beuerberg they comforted me when American trucks suddenly drove up to transfer us yet again. I howled; I could not take any more. My face was still an open wound, and we had to travel on the back of an uncovered truck. In Allgasing we managed to get an eye specialist drummed up from somewhere because we had ophthalmodynia, inflammation, and practically everything else. And now here we are, sharing a room again.

The "weather prophet" has his bed directly under the window facing the street. No more than a strip of lawn with a few shrubs separates the hut from the roadway—oh, and a fence. The fact that we are prisoners of war—there is a GI at the gate wearing one of those white helmets that look so strange to us—is not really at the front of our minds. The fence is only waist-high, made of crossed slats—what the Bavarians call a "hunter's fence."

Recknagel usually gets up this early and inspects himself in the mirror. Only his mouth and eyes still show traces of the severe burns. Cheloids are forming on his upper lip and on his chin—those red, proliferous, shiny scars that have no pores and pull your face out of shape. He stands there in his pale blue hospital outfit, craning forward, his breath misting up the mirror, feeling them with his index finger. Then he leans back, and is still for several minutes.

Walking on tiptoe in order not to wake us, he then goes over to his locker, reaches for the white shoebox containing his "field rations," and carefully takes it down. This is a daily ritual: the inspection of Recknagel's provisions. Removing the lid of the shoebox, he lowers his nose to the bread cubes stacked with meticulous symmetry inside and gives them an audible sniff. His pointed fingers, poking the stray cubes back into place, pick one up to test its consistency ("Got to be hard as iron. Fantastic nutritional value. I may be days slogging through the forest before I make Plauen . . ."). With a final, proprietary look at his precious store he replaces the lid on the box and the box on top of the locker.

He goes back to the mirror and starts cropping his beard with a pair of nail scissors, the skin on the wounds still too new and sensitive for shaving. The scars run like tight cords from the root of his nose to his chin. Healing is by no means complete, and it will be months before all movement stops in the disfigured face.

Meanwhile the rest of the hospital has woken up. The walls are thin, and I can hear them out in the corridor trudging to the washroom, hear the voices, hear taps turned on and doors slammed. I have gotten used to being a patient, being waited on. My hands are thickly bandaged, only the fingertips projecting from the fat, white bundles of cottonwool and gauze so that I can use them for scratching. This is important, because my face, and in particular my forehead—also bandaged—itches all the time. The gradual formation of new skin on the completely raw flesh is an unpleasant enough process in itself, tingling uninterruptedly as if a column of ants were crawling over the wound. But added to this the smell of pus and discharge attracts flies. Some weeks ago, when the pain was at its worst, with tetanus setting in and my resistance apparently about used up, I had hallucinations that turned me into a bundle of nerves and terrorized my surroundings. At night I thought I was being attacked by ants and gnats; grey swarms of them were creeping up my neck under the bandage. The nurse who sat by my bed during that time, when the tetanus was giving me spasms at almost regular intervals day and night, knew about my hallucinations and drove the imaginary vermin away, flapping at them with her hand ("Now you'll be all right—not a gnat to be seen. They'll leave you alone now and you can sleep.").

Nurse Leonie comes in with the washbasin and the kidney dish that she holds under my chin while I clean my teeth. She is a Red Cross nurse, formerly stationed in Upper Silesia where she went to school, now stationed here, Upper Silesia being lost. She has been without news of her parents and relatives since Breslau fell—"if they're still alive, that is," she says. She likes to talk as she washes me. She chatters away nonstop, and we let her chatter because she is our one source of information about the world beyond the fence. They have a wireless in the nurses' quarters, and being a member of staff rather than a patient (read: prisoner) she gets into Munich occasionally. Not that she enjoys it ("You can't conceive what the place looks like!").

To my surprise I am not in the least unhappy about my helpless condition. In any other condition I would only be transferred to an ordinary POW camp. The officers are still in the camps, particularly the higher ranks and all the general staff officers. ("All general staff officers are to be deported—to some island," Leonie told us. "I'm sitting pretty then," I said. "I'm only a line officer." "No," she said, spoiling my fun, "all colonels too—I heard it on the wireless.")

Now Holzamer is awake as well. That is to say, he has let it be seen that he is awake by stretching and at the same time giving vocal indications of relish. He passes his right hand—also destroyed by fire and now crippled—over the corners of his mouth and sucks in the saliva with a smacking noise, because the corners of his mouth do not close. No longer alarmed by the sound, I recognize it as a preliminary to speech. But Leonie forestalls him: "About time too, Mr. Holzamer. They'll be wanting you to fetch breakfast soon and you haven't even washed."

"Good morning," says Holzamer, maneuvering himself awkwardly into a crooked squat on the edge of the bed. He looks at me: "What's the program for today, *Oberst?*"

As soon as we realized that the Wehrmacht no longer existed, or rather that it was reduced to the populations of large numbers of POW camps, we found our own solution to the problem of address. Our weatherman, "Chief Executive Officer of the Imperial Meteorological Service," became simply "doctor," in recognition of his academic qualifications, while Lance-Corporal Holzamer was promoted to "Mr. Holzamer." And to make due allowance for the change to democratization and demilitarization, instead of calling me "*Herr Oberst*" they called me simply "*Oberst*"—"colonel."

One day being very much like another except that it brings yet more dismaying news and only increases my doubts as to whether I really can call myself lucky to have survived (albeit in a pitifully groggy condition) five years of destruction and slaughter, there is no answer to Holzamer's question.

Nurse Leonie has told us about the horrors of the concentration camps. She brings us the first peacetime newspapers, which call our attention repeatedly and in detail to the disgrace of our nation: Auschwitz, Treblinka, Buchenwald . . . (As if we had not known—but it was unthinkable and we had simply closed our ears to it, there being "no alternative in the pursuit of ultimate victory.")

Thuringia is being handed over to the Soviets in exchange for Berlin. For me it is like a bridge being torn down, severing my lifeline to the last place I can call home. My home in Pomerania, where I had just a few happy months following my marriage, is already lost (no news of Ursula and the children since I flew up to see them in March). Now I cannot even go back to Thuringia where I was born.

Holzamer has pulled himself together at last and shuffled off to the washroom, not without a parting shot from the weather prophet: "You really must do a bit more for the community, Mr. Holzamer."

(The "community" is we three.) He is clearly enjoying this symbiosis with "doctor" and "*Oberst*" (the latter decorated, to boot), though he does tend to evince a certain satisfaction at being rid of the yoke of military subordination—when, for example, it is a question of doing something for the Oberst and the doctor that they might conceivably be capable of doing for themselves ("After all, we're all civilians now . . .").

Holzamer is the only son of a widow. He left school at sixteen to work in a bank, and in 1943 he was drafted into a tank regiment. There he did more or less what was expected of him, and toward the end of 1944, when crews were becoming pretty scarce, they hauled him out of the office and put him in a tank. He had a driving license, he showed a certain aptitude for handling tanks, and as a result, before he had picked up more than the rudiments of tank-driving technique and the tactics of armored warfare, he found himself in the driving seat of a "Tiger"—which for him was like the fulfilment of a boyhood dream.

The story of how he got his wound is the story of the tragedy that hit Upper Silesia in January 1945, when Soviet troops swept through the province like a tidal wave and the carts full of women and children were forced off the icy roads into the snowdrifts by the advancing tanks or crushed under their tracks.

"We'd driven into a village near Gleiwitz the evening before. It was a bitterly cold evening. The company had assembled and pushed east but we were left on our own, lost, with no infantry and no grenadiers—a patrol of six Tigers almost out of fuel, utterly forsaken in the middle of a vast, blizzard-swept plain. Earlier in the day I had caught a glimpse of the Gleiwitz radio mast and had been haunted ever since by the thought that this was where the war had started ('We've been answering their fire since 5 a.m.!'*).

"As dawn was breaking we sighted an apparently endless train of little carts and sleds drawn by half-starved horses—or by women and old men—coming toward us.

"'We must cover their rear,' said our platoon leader. 'We'll move up to meet them. Careful how you go—the road's very narrow.'"

*As Hitler broadcast to the nation very early in the morning of his attack on Poland (*J.S.*).

"We rolled toward them at walking pace. They looked so pathetic I could have wept. But their faces were radiant as they greeted us; we might have been angels. Now their troubles were over, they thought, or at least now they were no longer in danger of being overrun by the Soviets.

"As we pulled up in line ahead in the drifting snow beside the road our platoon leader yelled down at them so loud that his voice broke: 'Get a move on, all of you—Ivan'll be here any minute! Hurry along there!' As they threw themselves forward, hauling on their straps and shafts and lashing their horses, they did not hide their disappointment at being bawled out by their own tank crews.

"It was a bright night even with the snow falling thickly and the wind whipping the flakes almost horizontally over the fields. The refugees had wrapped shawls round their faces and these were white with driven snow; the windward flanks of their scrawny beasts were coated with ice.

"I revved the engine of my Tiger to warm up the cab. My commanding officer was up in the turret hatch with the night glasses, scanning the fields and the road as far as the point where it disappeared over the brow of a hill to the east. Suddenly a colossal explosion threw me forward against the instruments and the armor plating in the vision slot. When I turned round the C.O. was lying in an unnaturally distorted position on the floor, having slid off the swivel seat. Shells were exploding in our immediate vicinity and the tank in front of us was on fire, throwing a ghastly light on the scene. We were not hit ourselves; the explosion had only knocked the C.O. out for a moment. The radio was squawking away incomprehensibly but I had lost my headphone. I clambered out of the driving seat and pulled myself up through the turret hatch to get my bearings. Chaos had broken out around us. The refugees were scattering in panic. With the burning Tiger effectively blocking the road they tried to get round it over the snow-covered fields. In the red glare of the blazing monster I saw them dancing like ghosts through the drifts, slashing wildly at their horses as the carts and sleds sank into the snow or toppled over, and then abandoning their possessions to concentrate on saving themselves.

"Staring at them, I realized that I could hardly hear anything. The first shell must have burst both eardrums. So that when the patrol leader's Tiger was hit I only saw the flash; the explosion was no more than a harmless thud in my ears. The engine of my Tiger was still running and I was just thinking that I must do something when the loader tugged at my trouser leg. I bent down to see what he wanted— and that was when it happened.

"The shell must have hit the side of our Tiger. It was as if someone had tossed a rock against the armor plating—and suddenly I was in the middle of a blazing inferno. My hands still gripped the turret rim. I hauled myself up, managed to pull my legs up after me, and found myself standing in the middle of a mass of flame. I made a blind jump off the top of the tank and landed in a sprawl on the icy road.

"Now the shooting and the hullabaloo around me were like something that was happening somewhere else. The crew of tank three dragged me out of reach of the flames, strapped me on top of their tank behind the turret, and after a dash through the throng of fleeing people and vehicles brought me to the dressing station. Theirs was the only Tiger of the patrol that had not been hit."

At around eleven o'clock Fräulein Kleinschmidt, the physiotherapist, arrives to try and restore some movement to my cervical vertebrae and the joints of my fingers. She does so very carefully because it hurts and because too much of a good thing could in this case be dangerous.

I believe she is very pretty, but since I see everything as if through a pane of frosted glass I can only answer for the oval of her face, her ash-blonde hair, and the sun-bronzed skin of her arms. She is small and agreeably plump. Holzamer has told me exactly how to "see" her: "Very nice, only not my type. She has masses of freckles. Also you can bet anything she's a slut. Every weekend she hitchhikes to Garmisch or somewhere up in the mountains—with Amis." Why does little Kleinschmidt stay on in this cheerless army hospital? Her home was "in the east." Here she has board and lodging. In any case there is not much sense in earning money anywhere else. She is undoubtedly waiting for a chance of a hospital job abroad. She also has a soft spot for soldiers, for these men whom the war has so knocked about. She lived with them on the Reich's farthest fronts, she understands the way they talk—perhaps, too, she is not unapprehensive of what awaits her abroad. She is not the only one here.

Kleinschmidt is helping us cautiously to reassemble our shattered picture of the outside world, at least as regards the "Amis" (the

Americans), life in the big city (Munich), and the genius with which
the Bavarians are coping with the end of the Third Reich.

It is from her we learn what curious birds these "Amis" are, how
they saunter about in patent-leather shoes with their snazzy made-to-
measure trousers ("tight as drums over the behind") always ironed to
a knife-edge. Their favorite pastime seems to be doodling through the
Upper Bavarian countryside four to a jeep sporting shiny helmets in
the most impossibly gaudy colors.

We find it hard to believe that they are "nice boys" who go round
doing a good-natured rich-man act with cigarettes, tobacco, pow-
dered milk, and similar luxuries. Except for the sentry at the gate—
and the gate is a long way from our hut—we see hardly anything of
them.

Kleinschmidt has also told us about the total devaluation of money
(we have none in any case) and how the country has reverted to
the barter system of our Germanic forebears. Cigarettes, eggs, milk,
butter—these have become hard currency. Food, the principal link in
the chain of exchange, is controlled by the farmers and smallholders,
and they—who can blame them?—are evidently driving a hard and
tricky bargain.

Once Kleinschmidt has gone I am reduced to "killing time," as
Holzamer puts it. I cannot read because I cannot see properly, and I
am not yet strong enough for long walks, added to which the bright
daylight gives me stabbing pains in the eyes. Holzamer enjoys keeping
me amused. The doctor usually sulks by himself in a corner, but Holzamer is insatiably curious; he wants to know exactly how it was—
"from eyewitnesses." "What was Göring really like—was he just idle
and callous? I mean, in 1918 he came home as a *'Pour le Mérite'*
pilot—rather as you've come out of this war with your Swords, *Oberst.*" Or: "Wasn't everything in this war betrayed to the enemy by
our own people? The bastards just let us bleed to death, didn't they,
while they looked after number one?"

The weather prophet usually maintains a moody silence in the face
of Holzamer's persistent questions. He has never really left the world
of the Führer's headquarters, and he has only reluctantly given up
defending the Third Reich brass because he had little with which to
counter my uncontrollable outbursts of loathing against those potentates. When he made the mistake of showing round his gold pocket
watch ("Given me by the Führer in person—for my hundred-per-cent

accurate weather forecasts before the Norwegian campaign") he un-
leashed the full force of my fury: "And did you also accurately forecast the fact that soldiers with no winter equipment, no gloves, and
no coats were bound to die a miserable death in the Russian winter?
Did you, doctor, seek to persuade him of the wrongness of making
the success of the Ardennes offensive almost exclusively dependent
on two weeks' bad weather—the most undependable factor of all—
and that his doing so made the whole offensive yet another crime in
the series of irresponsible strategic victories, so-called, for which we
had to thank the 'genius' of the Führer?" He defended his position
weakly at best, and now he is increasingly concerned to avoid any
commitment.

But Holzamer keeps nagging away. Might we still have won if the
jet fighters had been engaged concentrically and in time, and if so
ought we not to have acted earlier, mutinied, forced a showdown,
even shot? Mutiny, a showdown, perhaps a shooting—the very terms
we endlessly kicked around ourselves after the disgraceful outcome
of that so-called Areopagus* at the end of last year, 1944, before
finally deciding to fly out to see Generaloberst von Greim. By "we" I
mean the small group of officers of the Jagdwaffe, the Luftwaffe's
"Fighter Command," whom Göring subsequently, at the height of the
drama, reviled as mutineers, agitators, and traitors. Holzamer has
grasped exactly what the issue was: should we in the Luftwaffe have
staged our own 20 July? I do not know. All I know is that that whole
slice of my experience shortly before the crash lies undigested below
the threshold of consciousness, and that during the long agony of my
sleepless nights my futile thoughts revolve perpetually not so much
around remembered combat situations or moments of fear as around
that crisis of conscience.

The eye specialist calls in two or three times a week. The surgeon
we hardly ever see. The doctors are overworked; they also want urgently to get home, to get back into civilian life before they "miss the
bus" and all the practices and hospital jobs are filled.

Dr. Stumpf was an officer in the Luftwaffe reserve medical corps.
He beat his hands together over his head the first time he saw me to
take a look at my eyes. I complained of increasing pain in both eyes
and hypersensitivity to light: "I wish I could sit in the dark."

*The highest council of ancient Athens.

"Yes, there's a proper little ulcer forming in each eye. Could turn nasty if we don't protect you from the light immediately."

So here I have been lying for the past three weeks, in this darkened barracks room with only Nurse Leonie and good old Holzamer to talk to. But Dr. Stumpf is extremely conscientious; he looks in every day, although he has long had a job at the University Eye Clinic, and he gives me a great deal of hope. "We'll patch you up all right. You've no idea what plastic surgery can do nowadays. Your eyes will soon be as good as new." It may not be what he really thinks, but it has certainly helped me get through these three dreadful weeks of pain and helplessness.

Shortly before sunset my companions and I usually set out for our stroll up the hill. The evening air is cooler, my eyes can take the fading sunlight, and the walk between the huts, along the narrow garden path, and up the hill is not too much for me. Holzamer takes my arm. We meet other patients out enjoying the evening breeze, dressed in the same blue-and-white striped hospital outfits as ourselves. Everybody knows the "facial burns"; we swap tidbits of news and talk about how bad the food is or what we have heard on the radio—but we do so with a certain reserve, because after all this is a prison camp and we will be here for some time.

Arrived on the hilltop, we go through the same ritual every evening. The "doctor" describes for the nth time the Bavarian landscape spread out before us. On a clear day you can see a very long way, and we are having a fine summer—as if to compensate for all the things we must go without.

Because of my eyes I am not able to enjoy the beauty of the view to the same extent as my companion, so it is only for form's sake that I join in the performance with which we proceed at this point to astonish the other patients. As soon as the crimson ball of the setting sun touches the horizon we turn our backs to it, bend double, grasp our ankles, and gaze at the spectacle through our legs, accompanying these contortions with profuse expressions of approval and acknowledgement: "Yes—now I see it," "Fascinating!" and the like.

What we are admiring is a natural phenomenon. The tradition goes back to one evening when, watching the sunset from the top of our hill, we noticed that the weather prophet had launched into a curious gymnastic routine and asked him whether he perhaps had a touch of the sun. He proceeded to wax eloquent on the subject of the spectrum, on the imperfection of the human eye, and on the possibility of isolating the colors in accordance with the law of spectral analysis by "standing on one's head or looking through one's legs"—at sunset, of course.

Later—as late as possible to make the night less long—the nurse covers my eyes with soft cellulose tissue and binds an elastic bandage round my head. She resists (not always successfully) my pestering her for a sleeping drug. It is past midnight before I can get to sleep, and I am often plagued by terrible dreams. The nights are an unmitigated ordeal. I am not in the least tired, having spent most of the day in bed anyway, and I lie awake for hours. Everything that I put off thinking about during the day as belonging to the distant future ("Time to face that when I'm better") looms large and insoluble in the darkness.

One morning, having pushed the bandage up with my fingertips, I looked over at the next bed and thought I recognized Major Krupinski. We call him "the count."

"Yes, it's me all right, *Herr Oberst*. They brought me in last night. I'm glad we didn't wake you."

"Good God, count, where did you come from?"

"France—or rather England, with a short guest appearance in France. I'm a head case."

"What happened to you? What do you mean—a head case?"

"Ah, sir, that's a long story. It started so innocuously and it ended with an almighty wallop. We were taken prisoner in Salzburg, and the Amis were fully aware of what a catch they'd made. They weren't at all rough with us—they weren't even particularly unfriendly."

"How did you end up in Salzburg?" I wanted to know, "and how is General Galland?"

"When the Americans reached the outskirts of Munich we had to evacuate Riem airfield. The only usable airfield left in the Alpine Fortress was the one near Salzburg. We moved the unit there the evening before the Americans reached it. We put all the jet fighters in a nice neat line and blew them up when the first tanks came into view. The general must have been taken prisoner in the hospital."

"And how did you get to England?"

"Before we knew what was happening we—that is, all the jet squadron pilot officers—were in a transport plane taking off for England. There they put us in an interrogation camp and started trying

to worm secrets out of us. They succeeded, of course—what was there
to keep quiet about now? We saw the general from time to time as
well as other high-ranking officers who were being put through the
same mill. The fact that we were adequately fed and were occasionally even issued with cigarettes, tobacco, chocolate, and Nescafé mis-
led us into thinking that the horror stories about the incredible things
that would happen if we lost the war had been nothing but propaganda. We soon found out how wrong we were. This after all was an
interrogation camp, and as long as we were of any use to British
Intelligence we were kept fed and pampered. Afterward, however, the
treatment became noticeably rougher. We had to pack up our stuff
at a moment's notice and were shipped onto an antiquated hulk in
Portsmouth harbor. We had gone to some trouble to present a respectable appearance in clean uniforms complete with epaulets. A few
of us—and this idiot was one of them—still sported Knight's Crosses
with Oak Leaves, etc., around our necks. Others had left their decorations off, either because they had 'thought better of them' as a result
of talk about the dubious nature of the military decorations awarded
by Hitler or because they had an inkling of what we were in for and
wanted to remain inconspicuous.

"We tied up in Cherbourg the same evening, and the gruff tone in
which we were ordered to line up immediately in rank and file with
our meager belongings ought to have warned even me. I was the first
to step onto the gangway, but before I did so I cast a glance over
the crowd gathered below. French soldiers were struggling to keep a
narrow path clear, and as we started the descent I was aware of the
amused astonishment on the faces of the throng. 'How about this for
a bunch of comical specimens,' they seemed to be thinking. As I
headed the column down the gangway dressed in full war regalia a
murmur ran through the crowd. People began to laugh and crack
jokes; soon the space between the warehouses and the ship was ringing with their laughter. 'Chin up, count,' I said to myself. 'You've got
to get through there somehow.' And on I marched.

"At the foot of the gangway a *poilu* barred my way with his gun
and shouted a question at me. I didn't understand a word. The crowd
was suddenly quiet. Before I realized what the soldier was doing he
had reached out for my Knight's Cross and was tugging at it. I tried
to stay on my feet but he pulled me off balance. As I fell forward, out
of the corner of my eye I saw a rifle butt swinging down at my head.

"I came to next day in prison camp. It was one of the notorious 'hunger camps'; we were given almost nothing to eat. We were real POWs now—stripped of our insignia, crammed into huts, and utterly at the mercy of the camp authorities. I lay around for several days, vomiting and showing all the symptoms of serious concussion if not a fractured skull, before they decided to pack me off back to Germany. The journey—on coal trains, in open trucks and with no medical care—was one long agony from beginning to end. How I landed here I don't know. It's a miracle."

Nurse Leonie has told us about the preparations being made for a monster tribunal in Nuremberg. With Hitler dead, Göring will be the most prominent figure on trial. Our talk keeps coming back to the person of the former Reichsmarschall;* press and radio are full of him too. Just as a legend quickly grew up around him when he "conjured up" the Luftwaffe in the space of a few years, now his behavior on being taken prisoner, his conduct toward the Allies, and his role among the Nuremberg accused are providing food for a fresh legend. The "Iron Man" appears to be living up to his name again. He is not identified to the same extent with the misdeeds of the Nazi leadership as the rest of the top-ranking prisoners. He is privileged to be referred to still as "Hermann"—even if he did on one famous occasion wager that his name would be "Meier."

"Before we left Berlin—the Reichsmarschall had not yet slipped away to the Obersalzberg†—the Allies concentrated a series of heavy air raids on the Reichshauptstadt. . . ."

The weather prophet still has these relapses. For him Göring is still "*der Reichsmarschall*" and Berlin "*die Reichshauptstadt*," the "imperial capital."

". . . One evening as we were on the way to the Führerbunker we were obliged to make a dash for a civilian air-raid shelter because bombs had blocked the street and others were falling in our immediate vicinity. The Reichsmarschall preceded us down the steps and opened the door of the dimly lit vault. You can imagine what the

*The rank of *Reichsmarschall* was created specially for Göring after the victories of 1940 *(Tr.)*.
†Hitler's "Alpine Fortress" headquarters near Berchtesgaden *(Tr.)*.

inside of an air-raid shelter in the imperial capital looked like at this stage of the war. They stared at him—women, children, and old men—as at an apparition. But they recovered themselves quickly, as Berliners do: 'Here, *Herr Reichsmarschall*, there's plenty of room.' And they squeezed up to make room, evidently honored by the presence of the man who had braggingly proclaimed that enemy bombers would never get through to Berlin—'or my name's Meier!'

"He sat down between two old ladies, and I can tell you he made quite a picture—ensconced there in his unbuttoned overcoat with its white silk lapels, gold tabs, and outsize epaulets, sporting that unique creation, the Reichsmarschall's cap (it was practically made of gold thread), grumbling good-naturedly and looking about him with a friendly smile. There was no trace of ill-feeling against him; almost as if he too had been a victim of the unavoidable they started to complain about the terror raids, and he reacted affably, cracking jokes and cursing their common fate in having to sit it out in this cellar. 'Things are bad, people, I know, but you must be patient . . .' or 'Depend on it—I'm doing what I can . . .' or 'The Anglo-Saxons will pay for this' were some of his empty phrases. But a feeling of almost domestic security had descended on the cellar, and he revelled in it. When the all-clear sounded they sent him off with handshakes and best wishes, and as we continued on our way to Führerbunker he was moved to remark that it was distressing, was it not, to witness what these magnificent people were having to suffer. It is hardly likely to have entered his head, of course, that he, the Reichsmarschall, as commander in chief of the Luftwaffe, was basically to blame."

This set Holzamer off again. What had actually been wrong with the Luftwaffe then, and why had we not been in a position to stop the terror raids? What would have happened if we had been given the jet fighters sooner and they had been flown against the bombers? And had Göring really been so utterly dim and incompetent?

Question after question, and not all of them I can answer. But now that I have the count to back me up I more and more often find myself describing the events of the recent past. Together we have started reliving those air battles over England, over Stalingrad, over Tunis—and yet all it is is therapy against the perplexity with which we face the future.

But most of the memories that keep coming back to me have to do with the so-called revolt of the fighter pilots, which was actually no more than a belated, all too belated, attempt to change things. Was it a case of "too little, too late"? And why so late? Because a soldier is bound by the law of obedience, I tell myself in reply, and because . . . and because . . .

One day, I decide, as soon as I can use my hands again, I will write it all down, because when you write something down it becomes clearer in your mind. Probably I shall never get around to it, because if I ever get to be halfway fit again I shall have my work cut out earning my own and my family's living.

No word from Ursula and the children. I met a soldier in June who was going to try and make it through to Saxony and I gave him a brief message for my parents in Leipzig, my mother-in-law in Mecklenburg, and Ursula in Pomerania: "I've been wounded—burns. I'm all right. Look for me in Bavaria through the Red Cross." But there is very little news from "the other side," from the Soviet-occupied zone; all we know is that things are terrible there and that they are having to struggle merely to keep alive.

One morning I found a distinguished-looking young man standing beside my bed who introduced himself as ex-Leutnant Kelch. I had got to know Kelch in the last few months of the war. He came back with one leg after a POW swap with the Americans. Badly hit during the battle for England,* he had had to bale out over the island. He was now working as an interpreter for the American authorities in Munich and had come to tell me that my things—two suitcases—were at his flat only a few minutes' walk from the hospital. He had taken charge of them after my crash. There was also a typewriter, he told me, securely packed in a wooden box. I could have the stuff whenever I needed it, although it might be better to leave the cases with him until I was clear of hospital and captivity. Kelch left his address and went.

The typewriter, a present from my father, tempted me immediately. It was an ancient, stand-up Remington, but if I started dictating my recollections of the last few months of the war now, I thought, Holzamer could take them down on the typewriter, using the two-finger method, and it would provide a useful distraction from our sterile ruminations.

*i.e., the Battle of Britain *(Tr.)*.

By the next day my decision was made: I was going to get it. The count would accompany me—or rather, I would accompany him, he being even shakier on his pins than I. If we climbed over the low slat fence immediately behind our hut I reckoned the bushes would hide us from the sentry's view. Holzamer and the weather prophet could help heave us over. Dress was a headache. I decided on uniform trousers and a blue Luftwaffe shirt, topped by my long black leather overcoat—a typical piece of fighter pilot's extravagance. The count had to make do with a flimsy summer coat that Nurse Leonie had procured from somewhere.

Word got around that we were "going over the fence." Not that this represented a major problem because the hospital is only formally a prison camp; the patients are all either seriously wounded or they are homeless "refugees," being from the other side of the demarcation line, as the eastern frontier is now called. It will not have occurred to anyone to think we might be trying to escape. They simply took a terrific interest in the fact that the two ace fighter pilots, the "head case" and the "facial burn" with the fat bandage round his pate, wanted to go over the fence—and would no doubt have taken an even greater interest in our being nabbed. Every window was lined with faces peering through the curtains, while others took up positions in the bushes to get a grandstand view of the operation.

It was in fact quite a performance getting us both over. And it had to be done fast. Leonie, Holzamer, and the weather prophet had built the thing up into a kind of major breakout that simply *had* to succeed. The count in particular had trouble with the low fence and sat down heavily on the other side, puffing and blowing while I tugged nervously at his sleeve to get him on his feet again. Linking arms to support each other, we set off at a modest pace down the road. We did our best to look like innocent citizens out for a walk in order not to attract attention. But, hardened as the people of Munich had become in the last few months to poverty and suffering, there was not a passerby that did not turn and look at us with a mixture of curiosity and alarm. The count staggered occasionally, and I started to perspire with the onset of faintness, but we were both thoroughly enjoying the feeling of being "free," of being "outside" and able to move about unhindered.

The road dipped into a valley and ran through a sort of park before we came to the house where Kelch was living. There was a bench in the front garden, and we sat down to recover our strength before ringing the bell. Leaning back against the wall of the house, we congratulated ourselves on our success. "I hope we make it back to the hospital—they're expecting us in an hour," said the count. And I said: "You'll have to carry the typewriter while I help you keep your balance."

All of a sudden there was an old lady standing in front of us, clutching a string shopping bag and staring at us in wide-eyed astonishment. Before we could say anything ("Wait—we've come to fetch the typewriter from Mr. Kelch") she had scampered off round the corner of the house and disappeared. "We must look pretty funny," we agreed. "If she's so scared she may not even let us into the house."

But just then she came back round the corner with an enormous chunk of bread in her hand, and on the bread, secured by her thumb, lay a magnificent slice of streaky bacon. She came straight up to me and held out this delicacy, observing: "Here—you'll be hungry," and "Dear God, have they made a mess of you." Again, before I could stammer out my thanks she had turned tail and disappeared the way she had come.

"Do I look as bad as that?" I asked the count soberly.

"Come on—you just look a bit funny, that's all."

"Thanks," I said. "Just look at that piece of bacon. But you'll have to go in and get the typewriter, count—she's terrified of me."

The bacon sandwich was delicious and I ate it there and then. While the count was inside I remember thinking about the future. My ideas were pretty vague. One thing is clear: my profession—regular air-force officer—is never going to exist again in this country. What will become of us high-ranking officers, us "heroes," once the darlings of the nation, is anybody's guess. The top brass are already busy clearing themselves, and it is bound to be the generation that actually fought at the front that pays the price. I am a qualified sports instructor but I will certainly not be allowed to work as one: I might militarize the country's youth. With my Swords I shall in any case be bracketed with that fanatical group of veterans who continued to risk their lives at a time when every layman could see that the war was hopelessly lost. I cannot even go home, my home being in what is now the Soviet-occupied zone. Are Ursula and the children alive? I wonder; did they seek refuge with Ursula's mother in Warnemünde or with my parents in Leipzig?

The count came tottering back with the wooden box containing the typewriter. "She was very nice," he said. "She wanted to know what had happened to you. She said it was terrible and that we should feel free to come back any time. And look—she's given me a bacon sandwich too."

We made it back to the fence on time—completely exhausted and ready to drop but proud to have accomplished our mission—and the others were there to help us over. They bombarded us with questions almost as if we had just returned from a dangerous expedition to an uncharted land, and we gave a full report of our experiences. They were right in a way, too—it had been an expedition.

Leonie has fetched paper and all the other necessaries from the hospital office. Holzamer has removed the Remington from its wooden case, placed it on the table beside the neat piles of paper, carbon paper, and flimsy and the special eraser, and wound a sheet of paper into the carriage. With rigid forefingers—the only usable part of his revoltingly crippled hands—he now starts to prod away at the keyboard, totally absorbed; at last he has found something productive to do, and he is glad that he can help me.

"It's OK, colonel—it works a treat. You can start right away. You dictate your experiences in the last few months of the war like you were going to—exactly the way you told it to us—and I'll take it all down on the typewriter."

"It's too late for today, Mr. Holzamer. The count and I are whacked. But we'll make a start first thing in the morning—that I promise you."

I have laid aside my decorations. I shall not put them on again until the German Luftwaffe starts to fight with the kind of dedication it fought with when I won them. This is final, however; the Jagdwaffe is going to give battle to the last man. Those are my orders and I shall see them carried out regardless. If it does not, it can go and join the infantry. The German people doesn't give a damn about the Jagdwaffe's losses.

Reichsmarschall Hermann Göring
Obersalzberg, 7 October 1943

I
Schönwalde
October–November 1944

We had been at the advance airfield in Transylvania only two days when the order came through: "Fighter Group 77 to proceed immediately to Schönwalde airfield where it will be engaged in Reich Defense."

The rumble of the front was already audible. The artillery battle had begun during the night, and the village was frantically preparing to leave. As I stepped out of my billet I saw heavy farmcarts being loaded with all the things people take with them when they have to leave home in a hurry. Trunks, boxes, and bedclothes were piled in precarious heaps. The villagers, stunned by the fact that they must now abandon this paradise that had for centuries been their home, stood uncertainly around the carts in the pale dawn light, holding their children by the hand. It was harvest time; in the front gardens of the neat farmhouses mallows, asters, and sunflowers bloomed in wild profusion.

I had been billeted in the forester's house, which stood at the edge of the trees. I saw the dispatch rider tearing up the straight road toward me.

"You're to take off straight away, *Herr Oberst*—the artillery will soon be bombarding the airfield . . ."

"Come on, Straden," I told my adjutant, and to the villagers: "Get going, and make as much speed as you can. They'll be here before long."

Whips cracked, and the powerful horses strained in their harnesses. The line of carts, accompanied almost exclusively by women and old men, lurched into movement. The women sat perched on the mountainous loads, their round faces framed by colorful headscarves, trying desperately to keep everything together—boxes, children, billowing bedclothes, and the hams and loaves they had stuffed into pillowcases.

"What do we do with Piefke?" Straden asked.

The forester had had a litter of flaming red short-haired Dachshund pups and when flight became unavoidable he had said to me: "Help yourself to one—I can't take them with me." I had picked out a strong-looking male with tousled ears who seemed to be the leader of the pack. Why I called him "Piefke" I do not know, but after I had bribed him with "pilot's chocolate" he appeared to take to me.

"We're only flying to Debrecen. He can sit behind my headguard. He'll be all right if we don't fly too high."

We overtook the line of carts, turned into the path leading to the landing strip, and came to a halt beside the Messerschmitts just as the first shells started ripping up the lush green grass of the field. Piefke let me squeeze him into the tiny space behind the bullet-proof glass shield, and when I turned my head I could see his wet nose and his huge, frightened eyes.

We had taken off in a hurry and I was beginning to form up and count my aircraft when I heard excited shouting in the intercom—warnings and orders of the kind you get when someone has made contact with the enemy or is in a dogfight:

"Klausenburg, over Klausenburg . . ."*

"Whoever has combat, give location of polecat, come in."†

Several excited voices answered me at the same time, but again all I could make out was the word "Klausenburg."

I ran a forefinger over the map spread out on my knee. We had the fuel to fly via Klausenburg, and we might just manage to arrive before the battle was over.

---

*German name of Cluj, Romania *(Tr.)*.
†*Iltis*—"polecat"—was our code word for "enemy" *(J.S.)*.

As the needle climbed to 4,000 meters I suddenly thought of Piefke, and having no idea how oxygen deficiency affected dogs I decided I had better not fly any higher.

The flight—we were six aircraft—slid in perfect formation over the blue, densely wooded hills and the fields gleaming yellow in the autumn sun. The air was still and cloudless. At irregular intervals the intercom buzzed painfully in my ears. Then the shouting died down, and by the time we spotted the crimson roofs of Klausenburg lying between the forests and the fields the battle appeared to be over. The only sounds in my headphone were the occasional crackle and click.

"Messerschmitts up to port . . ."

I forgot who gave the warning, but there they were—four, no, six Messerschmitts. They hauled round in a tight curve, swung into our wake, and started to come up behind us.

"Look out—you're under fire! The Me's are attacking!"

I jerked my head round, pulled my plane into a left-hand turn, and saw a Me going for the last pair of the flight with everything he had.

"Romanians . . . Look out—they're Romanians!" It was Fährmann's high-pitched voice shouting, and then I saw for myself that the planes attacking us bore the emblem of the Royal Romanian Air Force on fuselage and wings. They were the old Me 109E, the one we called "Emil," with the square-cut wings and tailplane and the rounded nose. I knew we had fitted the Romanians out with a couple of squadrons of them.

Their attack having failed, they did not stand a chance. And yet I found myself in a curious state of agitation. I was about to open fire on Messerschmitts, on pilots who perhaps a week before had still been on our side, flying with us! The others seemed to share my emotion. The shouting in my headphone became incoherent, the flight had broken up, and suddenly we were involved in an all-out attack. Piefke was forgotten.

As I flew in and fired my cannon the target's legs fell out and a cloud of white coolant burst from the radiators under the wings. The Me rolled over on its back and went into a nose dive.

I could still catch the odd phrase from the battle in my headphone ("Look out!"—"Pull up!"—"Kill!") but now I had to make time to Debrecen airfield or risk running out of fuel.

It was then that I remembered Piefke. I turned in my seat to find his great big doggy eyes fixed on me. Back on the ground, he let me release him from his prison. He was trembling all over.

And from then on he never left my side.

In the evening we sat around the table of the little farmhouse and ate, by the light of a flickering oil lamp, something Rieber referred to as *Bauernfrühstück*, "peasants' breakfast"—a Bavarian concoction of fried potatoes, diced ham, and scrambled eggs. Rieber was my orderly, mess cook, canteen manager—in a word, my factotum. He had been with me since the Caucasus, accompanying me to Stalingrad and then to Sicily, and he had made himself thoroughly indispensable.

The arrival of the order to transfer to the Reich had ushered in a mood of depression. We felt like travelers approaching the end of an adventurous journey. We knew what "Reich Defense" meant: after the vagabond years in France, Russia, Africa, and Italy we were on our way back to a bombed-out, anguished homeland where we would be hurled into pitiless combat with the streams of Allied bombers. We would be kept relentlessly in action.

Conversation dragged. The usual flippant tone had given way abruptly to one of sober, objective consideration. What would be the consequences for the Reich if the circle were to close and the fight continue on German soil? Would it be possible at least to prevent our cities from being destroyed? Could a miracle still save us?

My mind kept coming back to the events of that day. I saw the stunned and helpless faces of the women on those fleeing farmcarts; the peaceful village street in that luxuriant paradise of plenty; gigantic yellow pumpkins, sunflowers as big as wagon wheels, and the banks of autumn flowers. And I knew that our homeland would confront us with all the things we had so far strenuously ignored: anguished, poverty-stricken people in flattened cities, pallid faces and despair, flavorless ersatz food, coffee, milk, and meat "substitutes," ration books, wood-gas cars, and air-raid warnings.

Granted, we had a heavy period of uninterrupted action behind us. We had hardly drawn breath since the Allied landing in Sicily. We had been dispatched like a fire brigade to every major conflagration on the southern front, been thrown back to France to combat the Allied invasion, and were now—after a guest appearance of a few days in Romania and Hungary—recalled to Berlin to take part in the defense of the Reich.

"But surely they'll let us have a few days' rest!" protested Straden. "We need aircraft and pilots, and we need to fly ourselves in against *Viermots**—we'll have forgotten how to do it."

"They don't go by the book much back home," said Hans Krug, our operations room officer. "Things are pretty rough and ready there. The Reichsmarschall's temper hasn't improved any since he wanted to have us court-martialed in Sicily for cowardice in the face of the enemy. He puts the whole blame for the Luftwaffe's failures and defeats on the Jagdwaffe. As soon as the Führer criticizes him he turns right round and points at us: 'It's them—they're the ones who've let us down. They're cowards.' He's given up wearing his decorations. Ever since Galland handed in his Knight's Cross Göring's had no choice but to go around himself in a plain dove grey uniform with no medals in order to show solidarity. But then he had his homilies to the fighter pilots recorded, if you please, and sent the records out to the groups. Those speeches were a mass of libellous insults woven round the monotonous theme: 'It's your fault, you're to blame!' He's not gotten any better aircraft so he sends us gramophone records of pep talks!"

Perplexity was written on every face. These men were suddenly going home, back to the Reich. They had lost their excuse for indifference ("We're at the front—we haven't time to share your worries. We're up there in combat almost daily."). They knew that flying fighters against bomber formations was murderous work, that they would never be safe again—either in the air or on the ground—and that nothing short of a miracle could see them through.

"But why don't they give us the jet fighters, for God's sake—the Me 262?" Fährmann wanted to know.

"Because Hitler still believes in the offensive against England and is coddling his bombers in the hope that one day he'll be able to use them in retaliation. . . ."

The three wings of Fighter Group 77 were stationed on the outskirts of the capital. The group staff and one wing set up in Schönwalde to the north of the city. It turned out to be an unexpectedly passive, almost peaceful time for us, that October. If it had not been for the continual air-raid warnings during the night and the fiery glare over Berlin one might have thought the war was over.

---

*Our slang for the Allies' four-engined ("viermotorige") bombers *(J.S.)*.

Galland, as "General of Fighter Pilots" the head of the Jagdwaffe, was building up his great "Fighter Reserve"—a force of 3,700 fighters with which to "strike the decisive blow at last" by shooting one complete raid out of the sky. We were given large numbers of new Messerschmitts. We were assigned young pilots who were timid, inexperienced, and scared. We flew little (fuel was in short supply) but were able to practice some formation flying and formation attacks on mock bomber flights. The young pilots were not yet ready for combat. It was hard enough leading and keeping together a large combat formation of experienced fighter pilots; with youngsters it was hopeless. They were just windy. They were expected to fly in precise formation, stuck in the middle of an enormous unit made up of more than a hundred fighters, keeping distance, height, and spacing constant. They were supposed to watch their air space and not let themselves be lured into dogfights with enemy fighters (they had absolutely no experience of aerial combat), and when the formation attacked the bomber armada they were told they must keep in position—come what might. It could never work. We had a lot of mechanical headaches too; practically every day someone turned back because of "motor running unevenly" or "spark plug trouble" or "low oil pressure."

The first women engineers, mechanics, armorers, and radio technicians began to report for duty to fill the places of the men who were needed at the front. The squadron's chief mechanic started grousing about discipline. His female ground staff were a little too susceptible to the advances of their male colleagues. Particularly the pilots took quite a fancy to the attractive assistants in snugly fitting black overalls who leaned down into their cockpits to help them on with their belts.

We found it difficult to get used to conditions in the Reich. Although we had not exactly lived in luxury in Russia and Africa (I remember the horseflesh with frozen potatoes in that winter before Moscow), Italy had more than made up for it. There we had shut ourselves up in an ephemeral world that looked no further than the next mission. All right, we read the front newspaper and we listened to the Wehrmacht news bulletin—but home was somewhere a long way away.

Now, however, our menu was the simple one dictated by scarcity and rationing and we had to surrender coupons for it. The propaganda spouting from the radio sounded eerie, unreal—and was inter-

rupted at almost regular intervals by "early warning," "pre-alert,"
and "alert." We had shut our ears before; on the (shrinking) periphery
of the Reich we had kept our eyes turned "frontward" and suppressed
our anxiety about the fate of our country with the therapy of combat,
attack, and the daily risk of death. Now there was no ducking it any
longer.

But our high command had given us a new goal: "This is where
you have to keep your nerve. . . . We're going to have to take a bit of
punishment and we mustn't let ourselves be drawn into dissipating
our energies."

So, ignoring the bombers, we flew and flew and practiced and practiced—and in the end we believed ourselves in the "decisive blow."

Around the middle of November a telex ordered me to attend a two-
day discussion "under the chairmanship of the Reichsmarschall" at
Gatow airfield in the western outskirts of Berlin. All highly decorated
unit commanders were to be present.

The conference room was a copybook example of the "Third Reich
style," plainly furnished with a table and chairs of pale stained beech.
A giant photograph of the Reichsmarschall wearing his Roman em-
peror's cape glared down at us. A bronze bust of Hitler stood on a
slender socle in the middle of one of the long walls, flanked by windows that admitted the late-autumn sunshine. A couple of engravings
in narrow frames—Frederick the Great and Moltke, familiar to all of
us from our officers' messes (they were mass-produced!)—stood out
against the pale wallpaper. Hideous lamps set in massive hexagonal
wooden structures intended to convey an impression of earthy rustic-
ity hung from chains above our heads.

We stood behind our chairs, waiting for the Reichsmarschall to
arrive. We were a distinguished company, "heroes" to a man, our
faces known to the whole nation from having been given endless ex-
posure by the propaganda machine in the pages of the illustrated
magazines and on the weekly newsreel. Good-looking, mostly very
young men. The autumn sun glinted off the decorations we wore at
our necks or on our chests. A hand-picked company, too—the most
bemedaled officers of the Luftwaffe, including the heads of bomber,
fighter, and reconnaissance commands.

I was between Lützow and Galland, the General of Fighter Pilots.
The general was wearing his uniform tunic in a stylish variant that

was clearly a product of his own imaginative ingenuity (or was he copying the Reichsmarschall?): it was done up at the neck in such a way that the white rank tabs adjoined, like the army tabs. But he wore no decorations.

I could not take my eyes off his profile as he stood there beside me, staring straight ahead of him with stoic calm. His face struck me as so intensely masculine, almost brutal, that for a moment I felt something of the sheer force of attraction the man exerted (on women in particular). His thick black hair (not a bit Germanic!) was combed straight back and lay like a helmet over his finely shaped skull. The forehead, the swayback nose, dating from a stunt-flying accident, the bushy black moustache, the thick-lipped mouth, and the heavy chin added up to a picture of awesome (to some people, terrifying) power.

"Gentlemen—the Reichsmarschall!"

The voice of the General of Bomber Pilots tore me away from my contemplation. General P. stood stiff as a ramrod beside the door through which the colossal bulk of the Reichsmarschall now appeared. Moving with surprising agility, Göring made straight for his place at the head of the table.

"*Herr Reichsmarschall*—reporting the officers you sent for present in full."

"Good morning, gentlemen."

I could feel myself already succumbing to the magnetic attraction of the man's voice when Lützow whispered from my right: "Play-actor! So it's dove grey today, is it?"

It was. He had on the dove grey uniform (double-breasted: the Reichsmarschall's privilege) with the broad white-silk lapels and—to my disappointment—long trousers. I knew him better in breeches and red Russian-leather boots, a sight that never failed to fascinate me by its sheer, unmitigated ugliness. Squeezing his vast backside between the armrests, he carefully lowered himself into his chair. Already the broad, determined mouth was open and the stentorian voice began to fill the room.

"Gentlemen. Though I call this gathering an Areopagus its purpose is not, I repeat not, to pass sentence with potsherds. I expect you to be my most fearless and successful soldiers. I further expect you to discuss in a critical manner anything in our service that may not—in your opinion—be satisfactory and that ought to be improved. Your criticisms, however, are to stop short of the head of the Luftwaffe—

your commander in chief. Discussion of this point is superfluous because *habemus pappam.*" And he repeated the words *habemus pappam,* laying a fleshy hand on his breast and showing off his rings.

"I want you to help me give the Luftwaffe back its reputation. The German people expects that, because we have failed—failed disgracefully. This is the Luftwaffe's darkest hour. The nations cannot understand why it is that the Allied bombers can come waltzing over the Reich as they did on the very day of our party congress and the fighters do not take off—because of fog, or because they are not ready, or because they are indisposed. . . ."

I know it by heart, I thought; I know this litany backward and forward, and I can't stand hearing it again.

He was getting worked up. His cheeks had turned pink and his eyes, which always looked too small for that vast expanse of face, were starting to glitter. It was the man's mouth that had always intrigued me most, that enormous vigorous mouth above the brutal chin. The lips were narrow and drawn in at the corners. A resolute mouth, but at the same time a sensual mouth, the mouth of a *bon viveur*—which, when it opened, revealed flawless but disproportionately tiny teeth.

And then he began the moaning and complaining, the praising and the flattering that were his all-out effort to channel the forthcoming "free discussion" along the lines he wanted it to take. He deplored the Luftwaffe's dwindling morale. In particular he forbade any repetition of "fruitless wrangling" regarding the question of whether the new jet aircraft, the Messerschmitt 262, should be used as a fighter or as a bomber since his decision to give the plane to his vastly more experienced bomber pilots was already of long standing. What does that leave worth discussing? I wondered.

Then he switched abruptly to a few timid fanfares: "We are on the threshold of the battle that will win us the war!" and "They ('our enemies') have problems too." And as if he had been a fire extinguisher that, having laid a thin carpet of foam over his audience, still had a little spurt in store, he raised his voice one last time to say:

"I regret that my commitments prevent me from leading the discussion in person but I am aware that in asking the General of Bomber Pilots, General P., to take my place I am leaving you in the best possible hands. Before I go, however, I should like to break the news that the General of Fighter Pilots has been promoted to the rank of Generalleutnant. My dear Galland, I share your delight."

Chairs scraped back and hands were offered with cries of "Congratulations!" Galland put a brave face on it and jovially shook the hands. But turning to me he muttered: "Bad sign, that—means it won't be long now before they sling me out."

In the general commotion hardly anyone had seen the Reichsmarschall leave the room. As General P. opened the meeting Galland lit up a long black Brazil and, at this signal, matches and lighters flared all the way down the table. It was like the beginning of a sit. discussion at one of the big staff HQs. The heads of fighter, reconnaissance, and bomber commands reported in a few words on the situation in their respective departments. They were matter-of-fact reports, and they were largely devoted to the weaknesses, the stoppages, the things that were no longer functioning. And a lot of things in the Luftwaffe and in the whole Third Reich were "no longer functioning."

They ducked the question of aerial defense. The night fighters were doing more than their stint, but they were short of aircraft and their organization was in a bad way. And daytime fighter defense against the mass attacks of the four-engined bombers was so hopeless a prospect as to be hardly worth talking about. The ban on discussion of the Me 262 made things even more futile.

Overriding the grumbled opposition of the Jagdwaffe officers, the chairman managed to put up for discussion the idea of a new and dynamic offensive in the air. The notion of bombing "the island" on the principle of "an eye for an eye" appeared—four years after Coventry—to have lost none of its fascination. It was as if the Allied bomber offensive filled them with envy. They refused to accept the fact that the Allies had just about perfected the use of air power as a weapon of attack. The thirst for retribution gave the discussion new momentum. It was almost weird—like a kind of shadow-boxing—the way they started talking about a couple of squadrons of Heinkel or Junkers bombers and how they were going to penetrate the antiaircraft defenses and strike the English cities and ports.

We knew, every one of us, that nothing could be done that would make any difference, nothing that might have diverted the ineluctable course of events. The bomber crews that had succeeded in penetrating to the heart of the island were undoubtedly the bravest of the brave.

And if they were lucky enough to come back it was with stories of an air-defense system so dense and deadly as almost to defy belief.

Even had a tentative effort been made to build a proper aircraft—a long-range four-engined strategic bomber—it would have been too late. In any case the technology was lacking, and the number of finished aircraft would never have gotten beyond two figures, whereas a single raid against the Reich was flown by a thousand and more British and American bombers. As for the fighters capable of escorting a German bomber formation to the island and back, they simply did not exist. The Jagdwaffe was not even capable of providing effective air defense over the Reich.

Yet they talked of an "O.C. England Offensive" as if there really were a commander somewhere who had the air power to strike blows that would tell and who was just waiting for the order to let loose.

We fighter pilots, a tiny minority among the participants in this "Areopagus," were following the discussion in a mood of baffled amazement when suddenly, before we realized what was going on, a fresh discussion point lay before the meeting: "Political commitment . . . permeation with National-Socialist ideology . . . faith in the Führer and victory . . ." We were to set ourselves up as an example to the nation in order to combat political indifference and lethargy.

A so-called National-Socialist Guidance Officer* attached to bomber command began to talk in moving terms about his work among various bomber units and in connection with the political-instruction courses at Oberjochberg, the bomber pilots' recreation and training center above Kitzbühel in Austria. He enlarged on the need for understanding, correctly interpreting, and uncompromisingly defending the ideas of National Socialism. The situation of the Reich was critical, he had to admit. But then again it was not—provided that the men who flew and fought identified themselves completely with the Führer's aims. Looked at in this way, there was no such ting as bravery in the abstract. Bravery was only inspiring, convincing, effective, and wholly honest when it stemmed from a deep-seated commitment to National-Socialist goals.

Raising his voice now, he told us he saw before him two fundamentally different types of combatant: those who, imbued to the core with

---

*A post created by Hitler's decree of 8 January 1944 to "bring about unqualified ideological unanimity between government and officer corps" (J.S.).

the political maxims of National Socialism, strove for victory with fanatical dedication—and those who, though they flew their missions bravely enough, failed signally to evince the same degree of fanaticism as far as the historical mission of National Socialism was concerned.

I had never heard anything like it. I had been back in the Reich for no more than a fortnight after a trapes round one theater of operations after another. At the front any indoctrination had remained within tolerable limits. We saw a copy of the local front newspaper every now and then, but the *Völkischer Beobachter*, the party newspaper, hardly ever reached us. For the rest we were dependent on the laconic Wehrmacht bulletins. When the National-Socialist Guidance Officers were introduced they were not able to send us a trained man and we had to make do with our own Hans Krug, who had a better command of the terminology of National-Socialist propaganda than the rest of us. As an amateur, however—he had been a reserve officer in the NS Flying Corps—he failed to instill in us the requisite "cold hatred and fanatical dedication." We held our routine social evenings with the crews and "Hänschen" made a stirring speech in which he sought to persuade us that "the future belongs not to the destructive ideas of the 'Red beasts,' but the constructive ideas of our own philosophy." But usually the evenings degenerated into cheerful boozing sessions and we let them do so, feeling we had "done our duty."

Now, however, we realized to our horror that a group of officers had decided, after five years of war, to conduct a purge among the troops with the object of eliminating all those "whose past life and present conduct were not consonant with the National-Socialist type" and who did not "stand firm on National-Socialist principles."

We sat there petrified, but some of those present appeared hugely to enjoy the ensuing discussion of what they called "National-Socialist guidelines." Perhaps, though, for many it was simply an attempt to escape into a less concrete area of discussion than the desperate military situation—and then there was the added satisfaction of being able to censure others. Fanaticism took the place of hopelessness, and phrases like "faith in the Führer," "rootedness in National-Socialist ideology," and "irreproachability of character" fell without hesitation from people's lips. The Luftwaffe leadership, it was said, must be "combed" from top to bottom, and then someone even came out with the "National-Socialist soul."

Lützow had sat through it all in tight-lipped silence, his face a mask. He turned to me. "I can't believe it," he breathed, "—they're talking about us. . . . Look—now Wernicke's asking for the floor. I bet he's got a copy of *Mein Kampf* in his briefcase."

Wernicke—one of our commanders, a fighter pilot—was already on his feet. Planting both hands on the table, he looked round him with a self-confident air before starting to speak. Pink, freckled face; reddish hair combed straight back. "A great many young men pass through my flying school," he began—too loud—"a great many young men who come from the Hitler Youth and who cannot wait to get to the front. It is an astonishing and regrettable fact that their National-Socialist education has left almost no trace. They are very far from having absorbed its ideas. One can neither discuss *The Myth of the Twentieth Century* with them, nor are they any too sure of their *Mein Kampf*. I must also, however, bewail the fact that we are inadequately supplied with modern literature."

The room was silent. All eyes were on this man—as if their owners expected some special revelation from him. He was visibly flattered. He sat down, threw his shoulders back, sent a self-satisfied smile round the table, and went on: "I have evolved a method that the Luftwaffe would do well to introduce. At morning roll call I read the assembled troops a key quotation from *Mein Kampf*. Every officer, NCO, and soldier has a little notebook in which he jots the quotation down. Before the books are collected in the evening the men have to enter in them how, in the light of the Führer's words, they have spent their day—how they have done their duty."

Lützow, under his breath, to me: "It's not true—it can't be. . . ."

There were some embarrassed looks. Other reactions ranged from sympathetic attention to whispered approval ("Interesting idea—he's got something there"). Encouraged by this positive reception, Wernicke delivered himself of the crowning touch: "In order to bring the maxims of National Socialism to the notice of my young compatriots in as impressive a way as possible, I have had quotations from the Führer painted on the hangar doors in letters a meter high. The doors of the largest hangar, for example, read: 'I will! Adolf Hitler.' . . ."

Some people absorbed even this with lively interest, and Wernicke looked around him with unconcealed pride. The rest of us exchanged looks of bewilderment.

The General of Bomber Pilots commended Wernicke's initiative, and it was clear that he now had the support of the majority. At this point, their imaginations having been so unexpectedly sparked off by a fighter pilot, they launched into an animated discussion of all kinds of ludicrous plans for cultivating political awareness among the "fighting force." And all of a sudden we had a new catchphrase: "the Luftwaffe creed." What was needed were convincing, inspiring statements of principle. Each and every individual must be committed to becoming a "fanatical supporter of the great historical mission of National-Socialist Germany." The conviction that, as the late Generaloberst D. had put it, "the tougher the situation, the greater our faith in the Führer" must as a matter of vital importance be carried into the very front line.

In a kind of frenzy of enthusiasm they appointed an editorial committee to draw up a stirring "profession of faith," sending them off into closed session where they could "devote themselves to this great and important task without danger of distraction." Our Wernicke did not need to be asked to place his experience at the committee's disposal.

We must have been there for hours already. With tedious monotony we had discussed operational methods and the shortage of equipment—and were not one bit the wiser. The taboo areas had remained taboo. The burning question "When does the Jagdwaffe get the Me 262 jet?" which the Reichsmarschall had expressly forbidden us to discuss, consequently remained unanswered.

We broke off for a pause and stood around the long table drinking coffee out of thick Wehrmacht mugs. The atmosphere had become chilly. Two camps had formed: the "politicals" were huddled in little whispering groups, and the "non-politicals" made it clear by the expressions on their faces that they hoped this farce would not go on much longer.

I felt a hand on my shoulder and turned to find myself face to face with Oberst S., who during the debate had vigorously taken up the cudgels for the "National-Socialist soul." We were the same age and had been through officers' school together.

"Do you fellows in fact realize," he asked, "that something has got to happen pretty soon? I mean that you're going to have to draw certain consequences as far as the higher echelons of the Jagdwaffe are concerned? We at any rate are disturbed by what we hear. Your behavior," he went on, clearly referring to all of us fighter pilots present, "your behavior, I mean the life you lead, these dreadful things with women in this difficult time—I mean it's appalling, isn't it?" There was a note of condescension in his voice.

I answered with reluctance, nauseated by the absurdity of the man's arguments. "Since you evidently include me, let me tell you that I fail to understand what kind of world you're living in. It is beyond me how you expect to win this war with ideological polemics. We at any rate fly aeroplanes and fight."

"Oh, you're just sore because the Reichsmarschall calls you fighter pilots a 'bunch of dead-beats.' What are you, then? What is this whole Jagdwaffe but a bunch of dead-beats?"

We were sitting round the table again and General P. was doing his best to get the exhausted discussion back on its feet when Galland passed me a note. It read: "Under pressure from the Führer the Reichsmarschall has given permission for the first jet-fighter group to be set up. Do you want to command it?"

My first reaction was to wonder why he bothered to ask. Did he think I was likely to refuse an offer like that? Then I thought: He wants to honor me. This is his way of telling me that he has confidence in me, that he thinks highly of me—his "thank you" for my efforts to persuade Hitler that this magnificent aircraft was a fighter and not a bomber.

I scribbled two words on the note and passed it back: "Many thanks!"

It had been four months earlier—the end of July 1944. We were flying missions against the Allied bombers from airfields in Upper Italy when I received the telex telling me I had been awarded the Swords pendant to the Knight's Cross with Oak Leaves. The citation spoke of consistent heroism, of a fine record of victories in the air, of exemplary fighting spirit. I was to report to the Führer's headquarters in two days' time.

We arrived at the "Wolfsschanze," Hitler's headquarters near Rastenburg (Polish: Ketrzyn), the evening before the appointed day— "we" being Leutnant B., Major S., and myself. It was very quiet. The huge rooms of the officers' home were almost empty, with only a few SS orderlies serving the handful of guests.

We sat out on the terrace in the gathering dusk. The sun as it slowly set threw a blood-red reflection onto the little lake below us. The forests were a pitch-black backcloth sweeping up to the purple sky. The occasional guest came out, stood stiffly to attention in the doorway with one arm raised in the so-called German salute—and beat a hasty retreat as soon as he became aware of the almost hostile emptiness of the place. The "German salute" had been compulsory in the Wehrmacht since the assassination attempt of a fortnight before. After some initial reluctance we had soon got used to this very far from natural way of showing respect for one's superiors. We had other problems.

This was my second visit to the "Wolfsschanze." The first had been in the summer of 1942, when Hitler gave me my Oak Leaves. On that occasion I had found an atmosphere of bustling self-confidence. The reverses and heavy losses of that first winter in Russia seemed to have been more than outweighed by the triumphal advance to the Caucasus, the crossing of the Don, and the virtually unopposed thrust into the Kalmuk Steppe. Hitler himself had played the conqueror, pontificating to us, very occasionally asking a question, and expounding this triumph and his plans for the future in a state of something like intoxication. He was going to improve the Reich's dwindling oil supplies drastically, he had told us, referring to Maykop and Baku. (But Baku we never reached, and I had just flown in from Maykop and knew that the Russians had poured liquid cement down the boreholds and that we would probably not get a drop out of them.) He had talked of advancing to the Black Sea and down the Groznyy military road to Tiflis. (But I knew that the mountain infantry's attempt to thrust through to Sochi on the Black Sea coast had got bogged down in the rain forests of the Caucasus and that we had begun to supply the advance units from the air, dropping tinned food and bread packed in hay bales.) Hitler's enthusiasm appeared to be shared by the whole operations staff of the Wehrmacht, so that I had left the "Wolfsschanze" in that summer of 1942 armed with the kind of moral equipment with which it was customary to send off the commanding officers of frontline units that were fighting a thousand and more miles from the frontiers of the Reich. I had arrived back in Maykop to find them already packing up preparatory to transferring to an advance airfield inside the great bow of the Don; our orders were to "relieve" the 6th Army, which had reached the Volga at Stalingrad—and was now cut off.

How the atmosphere at the Führer's headquarters had changed

since then! Two years ago the staff officers had been friendly, forthcoming; now there was almost none of that left. Shyly and as it were
apologetically they went out of their way to avoid us. So there we sat,
alone on the terrace, lost in our thoughts.

Only Major S. felt like talking. He told us how he and his flak unit
(20 mm four-barreled antiaircraft guns) had fought their way through
from Smolensk to East Prussia—boldly and "ruthlessly," as he put it.
("Anyone who's wounded gets left behind—we can only use healthy
fighting men.") They had broken out of numerous pockets to catch up
again with the retreating German army. The Russians were making
masterly use of the tactics of advance we had demonstrated so successfully on our entry into Russia in 1941. Overtaking the sluggish
and often undisciplined columns of German troops and their baggage
trains in wide-ranging pincer movements, they would repeatedly close
the circle and wipe out everything in it. Major S.'s description of the
retreat rivaled everything I had read about the ordeal of Napoleon's
Grande Armée after the Fire of Moscow.

"I shall tell the Führer about it in no uncertain terms," he said,
meaning the "bungling" of the general-staff officers and the "hopeless
corruption in the rear." "They had their carts piled high with Russki
women and eggs and hams—but I gave no quarter. Whenever I found
them blocking a road or a bridge or a ford I gave them a few minutes
to clear it, and if they didn't, I fired—right into the mêlée of carts and
bodies with my four-barreled flak guns. . . ."

Before we were allowed to enter Hitler's presence an SS officer told
us to take off our gun belts. We did so, and were shown into the dimly
lit reception room.

As he came toward me with left hand extended I saw with a start
that he had aged. He looked worn-out. It was the face of an old man,
the flaccid skin forming a network of folds around the mouth and
chin and the watery, almost muddy eyes seeming to stare into the
distance.

His voice was rough, like a chain-smoker's, although he spoke in a
subdued monotone. I noticed again how gutturally he rolled his r's—
and how effortlessly he phrased himself in the style of his speeches.

He could spare us only a few minutes.

"Please be seated."

We sat bolt upright—we might have swallowed sticks—on the

edges of excessively deep, modern leather armchairs and held our caps on our knees with both hands.

"You have come from Italy?" He had done his homework as usual. "And you from the eastern front? The front has come to a standstill. I found the mistake immediately. Kesselring will manage all right in Italy, but here in the Reich we must call a halt to this bomb terror. That has got to stop, whatever happens."

The army colonel who was standing beside Hitler bent down and whispered in his ear: "*Mein Führer*, your Luftwaffe adjutant, Oberst B., is away today. Shall I fetch General Ch.?"

Hitler stiffened, then let fly: "You'll fetch no one—no one, do you hear? I don't even want you. I want to hear the truth from my men at the front."

He turned back to us. "Are you inferior to the Americans with your Messerschmitts and Focke-Wulfs?" He put it as directly as that and with the implication: "I really want to know—I want the plain, unvarnished truth."

Leutnant B.'s answer was equally direct: "Yes, we are, *mein Führer*. The American and British fighters are between fifty and seventy kilometers an hour faster. They can fly higher, and they are more maneuverable."

"But you have these methanol-injection engines—I thought they were extremely powerful . . ."

"Even so, *mein Führer*, the others are faster."

"We need a new and better aircraft, *mein Führer*," I put in, adding, "I was thinking of the jet fighter."

He turned to face me, fixing those dead eyes on me. I had evidently broken a taboo because a flush came to his cheeks. The fingers of his left hand began to drum nervously on the table. "When will people stop trying to go behind my back and use my tried and tested front-line commanders to put pressure on me. . . ."

"*Mein Führer*," I hurried on, wanting to make the most of this rare opportunity, "I flew the Messerschmitt 262 a few days ago—it's a magnificent aircraft!"

His voice suddenly had a metallic, threatening edge to it: "I don't wish to hear any more of this nonsense! I've had enough of it! Fate hands me this one chance of wreaking a terrible vengeance—and here are you people trying to deprive me of it with short-sighted squabbles between bomber and fighter pilots. My decision is made. This aircraft is a bomber, a *Blitz* bomber—my instrument of revenge! It is not a fighter and it never can be a fighter."

I wanted to put in another protest but he cut me short with an imperious gesture.

"My doctor has solemnly warned me against trying to use it as such. This aircraft flies at speeds that not long ago we thought impossible. You fighters have to climb and dive steeply. You have to turn sharply—that's the whole secret of dogfighting. And that is just what you cannot do with this aircraft because the enormous accelerative forces set up during banking and pulling out induce disturbances of consciousness and even blackouts!"

Having begun in a fairly restrained tone, his lecture culminated in his trumpet blast. Here was the old self-assurance once again, the voice that swept aside all contradiction, the staccato, spat-out phrases of the speeches to the nation. I was stunned, although the tirade was not aimed at me. He was not even facing me as he delivered it but spoke as if to an invisible audience—whose reaction appeared to please him.

"When will you finally get this idea out of your heads! I don't want to hear another word about it! In any case, for you I've got something better—something tailor-made for the Jagdwaffe. You're in for a surprise."

I wondered what it could be. Was he perhaps right after all with his warnings about the effects of G forces? But that was all nonsense! You did not use this jet for dogfighting; you took advantage of its colossal speed to come up on the enemy unexpectedly and fire. Who had been feeding him this rubbish? What did his doctor know about it anyway?

We had listened in embarrassed silence. Not that I was intimidated by his rebuke, but I could feel disappointment welling up in me and I was waiting only for the moment when the voice would stop and he would dismiss us. Two years before he had set out his vast, unrealistic plans for us with euphoric gestures—the Caucasus, Tiflis, the Black Sea, the Caspian Sea . . . and oil, oil galore! Now, his outburst over, he sat there exhausted and listened to a report of the catastrophes occurring on the eastern front. He grimly shook his head as Major S. described the appalling butchery of the countless running engagements in the vivid language of the frontline soldier.

Then, as if he felt called upon to bolster up the morale of the

"front" as personified by ourselves, he launched abruptly into another lecture. He spoke of the German people that only showed its
true greatness in adversity, of the historical turning-point that lay just
ahead. (What does he mean by "turning-point," I thought, and how
far ahead?) He was confident of victory in the end as long as we—his
brave fighting men—did our duty. (Hadn't we been doing our duty
for the last five years?) And he had reliable information to the effect
that the Allies were demoralized. "The German people is capable,
when its back is to the wall, of incredible, magnificent achievements.
I shall astonish the world by mobilizing the entire nation in a way the
world has never seen before. I shall repay terror with terror."

I struggled back to the present. Lützow was saying with his tongue in
his cheek: "By the way, what's happening about our 'creed'?" General
H. suggested asking when the meeting would have a draft to discuss.
In the course of our tedious and unprofitable deliberations the "Luftwaffe creed" had almost been forgotten. In addition the committee
that was working on it appeared to be having difficulty over the
wording. The luncheon break on the second day went by without our
having been confronted with the fruit of their ideological efforts. It
augured badly for the forthcoming discussion that at the beginning of
the last afternoon of the "Areopagus" the draft was still not ready for
presentation. We were tired and by now there were few of us left who
were not convinced of the futility of this whole undertaking. There
was a general feeling of wanting to "break it up"—some were in a
hurry to get back to their units, which in this period of growing hopelessness offered security and the possibility of action as an antidote to
useless reflection; others wanted to return to their staffs and training
schools and bury themselves in work once more (work being another
kind of anti-thinking therapy). The fervent ideological hair-splitting
and aggressive witch-hunting of the beginning of the meeting had disappeared. They had gathered during the course of the discussion that
the "non-politicals" were capable of reacting fiercely and had no time
at all for political arguments.

Eventually, having spent more than a day ruminating, the editorial
committee returned to the conference room. They acted almost like a
delegation, arranging themselves around the head of the table while
copies of the proposed "creed" were distributed to the rest of us. So
there it was at last, in black and white: "We profess and believe . . .

for Führer and people . . . without thought for our own lives and until our dying breath . . ."

General Galland had given the sheet of paper no more than a cursory glance before laying it on the table in front of him. He sat there, chewing on his cigar. Lützow turned to me and, when I shook my head, leaned over and said under his breath: "They're crazy! Surely they don't seriously think they can inspire selfless dedication with party slogans like these. After all it's we pilots who are doing the flying and fighting. They're just trying to humiliate us. They want to humiliate us by forcing us to discuss this rubbish and give it our OK."

"It seems to me we should all have another good think about this. . . ."

It was Galland's voice, cool and detached. And as if they realized that this striving for political commitment had been so much shadow-boxing and that reality—bleak, terrifying reality—was not to be spirited away with doctrinaire phraseology, they capitulated, falling in with his proposal to "have another good think about it."

We parted with chilly farewells—and not without being treated to further assurances of how "necessary" and how "important" the occasion had been. Nevertheless I left Gatow with the feeling that I was heading for a dangerous and challenging episode in my career, and it pushed the depression of the last two days into the background.

I was to organize and command the first group of jet-propelled fighter aircraft.

2
Brandenburg
November–December 1944

Anxious to begin activating the first jet-fighter group as soon as possible, I rushed through the preparations for handing over Fighter Group 77 to my successor. There was no time for a farewell binge, no time for nostalgia ("Where are the old comrades—for two years we fought together on front after front . . ."). The ground and operations staff of the new group, Fighter Group 7, were already in Brandenburg, waiting for their commanding officer. The ground staff—the mechanics and armorers—were from a bomber group that had been wound up; the pilots came from flying school or from other fighter or bomber units. All in all it was a pretty bold venture, setting up a jet-fighter group and training it to fly against the big bombers at a time when the fronts were getting close to the borders of the Reich and the Allies were the undisputed masters of the air above it.

The three wings of Fighter Group 7 were based at Brandenburg, Parchim, and Kaltenkirchen, just north of Hamburg. The group subsequently came to include the experimental fighter unit that had been commanded by the late Major Novotny, the man who had done so much to prove that the Me 262 was a first-class fighter aircraft.

The first machines began to arrive. They came in sections on long railway trucks from the south of the Reich, and the mechanics, assisted by a team from the Messerschmitt works, started assembling them and shooting in the cannon. By the end of November we were in the air, training in flights of three and in small formations.

Meanwhile the Allied bomber offensive continued unabated. The raids on nearby Berlin woke us up with a start practically every night. We moved into quarters away from the airfield, fearing that so tempting a target—with hangars and parking areas full of jet aircraft—was bound to be attacked before long.

We could hardly have led a more unreal existence than we did in the few weeks that were necessary to fly the planes in and get the complex machinery of a fighter group running smoothly. Not only were we left in peace but our every wish—and a unit in process of formation has a great many wishes—was complied with. Perhaps it was partly the hope that a new and dangerous weapon was being forged here (the "miracle weapon") that led our superiors to pamper us in this way. We had time—time to play cards, time to talk, even time to go to the cinema, although air-raid warnings usually interrupted the performance. The city of Brandenburg was like the backdrop of a third-rate theater. Houses lay in ruins, the gardens were untended, and the peeling camouflage paint and shabby trams offered little temptation to hit town with our ration books and have a meal in a restaurant or a drink in a pub. We slipped into the privileged existence we were used to, spending our time in the officers' mess or in one another's rooms. We still had plenty to eat, plenty of brandy, champagne, and red wine, and plenty of cigarettes and cigars. And as if they had a sixth sense for these pleasures—and of course because they were attracted by these healthy young men, these national heroes, these pilots of the "miracle" plane—there were plenty of girls. They were no blushing damsels either and they did not want much wooing. They could take their drink, and they were as little bothered by their admirers' wedding rings as they were on the lookout for a permanent liaison.

The fitting-out of the group proceeded slowly. Assembling and flying in the planes was a time-consuming business, and there were hitches regarding parts and special components, as is often the case when you are introducing a new type. So it was all of six weeks before one had the feeling that a unit was taking shape—before, in other words, we were able to start proper formation training and I could at last report that, within limits, we were "ready for action."

The wing commanders who took the young pilots in hand and trained them were all successful fighter pilots with front experience but even they did not really have enough experience and against four-engined bombers virtually none at all. Only Novotny's old experimental unit—now the third wing of my group—had begun in numerous aerial engagements to work out combat tactics for jet fighters. They were an invaluable fund of experience.

Lützow—at that time commander of the 4th Division—came to see how we were getting on. He was impressed by the technical breakthrough represented by our having got this revolutionary aircraft ready for combat duty, and it was all I could do to restrain his euphoric outbursts to the effect that we were on the threshold of a new era in the battle against the four-engined bombers.

It was typical of Lützow that his moods were very much dictated by the way he felt at any one time. For example he could claim in an access of jubilant optimism that at last there was "a glimmer of hope"—and not long afterward be moaning in a state of the deepest despair that it was all too late, much too late and much too little. We talked about "air defense," but in fact there was nothing to justify the term; we had no defense. The British had developed their Bomber Command into a formidable instrument of mass destruction that could now reduce cities like Königsberg and Danzig to ashes overnight without encountering any opposition to speak of. The American 8th and 15th Air Forces flew over the Reich daily and were beginning, now that our energy supplies had finally been throttled by the destruction of the major synthetic-petrol refineries, systematically to wipe out city after city. Our fuel quota had been cut back drastically: we were hardly even allowed the minimum number of flying hours needed to train halfway competent pilots. But Messerschmitt fighters were being produced in hundreds and sent out to all airfields.

"What an opportunity, though!" Lützow enthused. "When you attack your first major raid of four-engined bombers in formation or at least with a number of Me 262s—and slaughter it—the Americans will get the biggest shock they've had since Schweinefurt!"

But we still had no combat tactics that we could lay down for our pilots. Discussion of the ideal method of attacking large, tight formations of four-engined bombers dominated our conversation—as it was to continue to do right up until the end of the war. We evolved a number of theories as to how best to fly the Me 262 against the bomber streams and were very far from agreeing on a common system. Even the experts in this type of engagement were at variance. Our strength lay in our enormous speed. The reaction propulsion generated by the new aircraft's turbines made us something like twice as fast as the enemy's airscrew-driven fighters. Moreover the armament of the Me 262—with four three-centimeter cannon—was not only sensational; it was also ideally suited to destroying the solid, "thick-skinned" bombers. But the technology of this revolutionary machine also had its weaknesses that made high-level aerial combat and attacks on bomber formations problematical. Swinging into the target's wake from above was out because of the danger of exceeding the maximum safe speed, the aircraft having no dive brakes with which to check the rapid acceleration involved in such a maneuver. Frontal attack on collision course with the bombers—a favorite method with the experts because the target was then virtually defenseless and the crews of the Flying Fortresses were exposed to the hail of bullets—was also out because the combined approach speeds made a considered attack impossible.

In practice we went back to the old, conventional attack from behind, approaching the bomber formation—with of course a tremendous speed plus—through the defensive fire of the rear gunners and letting off our cannon at short range. The Me 262 was a pretty sensitive and vulnerable piece of machinery, however, and our losses turned out to be higher than we had feared.

Lützow had some extremely alarming news about goings-on at the head of the Jagdwaffe. General Galland had not seen Göring for weeks. His attempts to have the Jagdwaffe made the sole focus of our air-armament effort had evoked no reaction. The intrigues about his person appeared finally to have undermined Göring's—and Hitler's—confidence in his continued fitness for the post of General of Fighter Pilots, and it looked as if his dismissal was only a matter of time.

Göring's campaign against the day fighters had reached a fresh climax. He now shamelessly put the catastrophe of our aerial defense down to a lack of fighting spirit on the part of the Jagdwaffe. The system of night fighters built up with enormous energy and technical know-how by General Kammhuber had fallen victim to Göring's failure to understand this complicated form of night defense, and Kammhuber himself had been shelved, so that the enemy could now safely attack by night as well.

We arranged that Lützow should let me know when things reached a head, since—and here we were in full agreement—all efforts would be in vain if the opportunity of mounting a concentrated air defense was wasted. Then nothing more would stand in the way of the final, systematic destruction of our country. And who if not we, as experienced commanding officers, was in a position to do anything about it? Lützow had told me he was on a similar footing with Trautloft, Rödel, Newmann, and others. We were well on the way to becoming conspirators.

Toward the end of November I received a message asking me to meet the General of Fighter Pilots next day in Parchim, where one of the wings of my group was organizing.

It was a rainy morning when I arrived in Parchim. The clouds hung low over the forests surrounding the airfield, and I was just beginning to wonder whether the general, who had announced his arrival by air, would be able to fly at all in such weather when the two-engined machine he used for traveling loomed like a shadow out of the sheets of rain and touched down on the landing strip. I knew the general loved a risky flight, but that performance had my unqualified respect.

Galland's face was dark and surly as I reported on the state of the unit. He growled a couple of questions, appeared to be anything but satisfied with my answers, and then abruptly gave vent to his ill humor by accusing me of not getting the unit on its feet fast enough and not acting rigorously enough: "Look—if you've not got the machines for your formations, Macky, the thing to do is to get your group flight fitted out first and show what this aircraft can do in action!"

I shot him an irritated glance and did not answer immediately, being familiar with his way of taking out his anger on the first available object. Then I said simply: "Of course I've got my group flight, *Herr General*—but I have in mind your own maxim that we should pelt rather than piddle."

He flipped a hand. "All right, forget it."

We walked down the taxi strip together, hardly exchanging another word except that the general said: "It's still the same— everyone's against us. I can't get to see Göring to talk to him. They're toying with the most fantastic ideas there—things that represent a complete reversal of all I regard as right and necessary. They all think they can tell me my business, but none of them with these farcical ideas about using fighters is prepared to give a practical demonstration—i.e., get his own arse up there!"

"But that means it's all over," I put in.

"I'm afraid it's been that for a long time, Macky. But how are we going to be able to show our faces before history—and I don't mean that pompously—if we look on without lifting a finger while this country and its cities are wiped out, knowing as we do that something can be done about it, that it can be stopped? . . ."

Later we shared a tasteless canteen meal with the pilots and took part in a discussion that centered—as our discussions had centered for weeks—on combat tactics against the bombers. To my surprise I found myself among men with a new kind of self-assurance. Those pilots were not only conscious of having been handpicked to fly in the first jet-fighter unit; they knew that with the Me 262 they were more than a match for any enemy. The result was a reawakening of the sort of fiery determination that had characterized the Luftwaffe in the early days of the war.

Climbing back into his aircraft afterward, the general turned and beckoned me closer. "It's best if I warn you, Macky," he said quietly. "You're on the black list. You'd better be a bit more careful about criticizing your superiors. The head of personnel told me in conversation that Göring's been saying: 'Steinhoff's another one who seems to be getting tired—I need younger, more positive men . . .'."

I said nothing. I could feel the anger rising in me and was at a loss for an answer.

"If it's any consolation," Galland went on, "I'm being shot down too."

Nor did December see much progress with the group. We were able to assemble enough aircraft in the hangars to bring the group staff and the Brandenburg wing up to strength and put us in a position where we could risk our first outing. But the December weather seldom came up to the minimum conditions necessary to fly the planes in. There was usually low cloud, visibility was reduced by fog, and the first snow showers swept across the airfield. To strike our blow we needed good visibility at the airfield, and the cloud cover must not be so thick as to prevent us climbing to the height of the bombers.

Flying through cloud to find bombers was difficult enough anyway; in December it was impossible.

The Allies were meanwhile flying day and night and completing their work of destruction. The General of Fighter Pilots, however, was determined to keep his head. His "Fighter Reserve" had by now reached respectable proportions, and he intended to decimate a major formation of four-engined bombers by a properly coordinated attack using prop fighters in conjunction with our jets. A difficulty here was the Me 262's limited range and flying time. On the other hand its climbing capacity meant that it could take off very late and, the bombers flying relatively slowly, could contact the enemy with great precision.

We reckoned to fly our first big operation in early January, since the winter high that usually sets in around that time promised the ideal kind of weather for our plan.

To enable him to make the best possible use of his fighter power while the bomber formation was in the Reich's air space Galland decided to move my group to the west of the country. The idea was that the jets should have first go at the enemy in order to scatter the fighter escort and shake up the bomber formation, thus making things easier for the prop-fighter groups of the "Fighter Reserve," which would attack farther east.

With the object of finding two or three airfields suitable for jet fighters I drove west a few days before Christmas to have a look at fields around Soest, north of the Ruhr district, and on the Lower Rhine. It was not a journey that held out any hope of things taking a turn for the better. The Americans had just started concentrating their attention on the Ruhr, and the gloomy picture of cities reduced to rubble and men to weary resignation gave me every reason to feel depressed.

Only once, as I was climbing one of those winding pass roads in the Westerwald and one of the new rockets ("My retribution!") shot up with a flash and a roar and disappeared in the low cloud, did I feel something akin to pride at the fact that, on our knees as we were, and with the enemy long fighting on German soil, we were still capable of this kind of technological achievement.

Driving back along the *Autobahn* between Helmstedt and Magdeburg a few days later, I ran into thick, yellow fog just as night was falling. The windscreen began to ice up, and I had to open the side window and drive at walking speed along the white line. I took the Magdeburg exit and had a terrible job finding the railway station in the blacked-out town, which around midnight looked completely dead. Leaving my driver to get his car back, I was lucky enough to catch a train that dropped me in Brandenburg early the next morning.

There I went to the station commander's office and put through a call to my group headquarters.

"Transport pool, please."

"Fighter Group 7 transport pool, Feldwebel F. speaking."

"Oberst Steinhoff here. Please send my car round to the station."

There was a moment's silence, then the sergeant began to stutter: "Er . . . *Herr Oberst* . . . the car . . ."

"Yes, what is it? I'd like my car. I'm dead tired."

"But the commander drove to Berlin in it yesterday, sir. I mean the new commander."

Well, Galland had warned me. After the first second of shock my indignation at this unseemly and underhand way of giving me the sack sharpened my reactions.

"Get me the switchboard."

"Right away, sir."

"Hello—switchboard, please give me my adjutant."

No explanation was necessary; everyone in the group had heard long before. I told Fährmann to get hold of some kind of vehicle for me—I just wanted to pack up my things in a hurry and get out. This time there were no buts. I drove straight to my billet, and while I recovered from my overnight journey over a good breakfast my batman Rieber started putting my things together. There was not a lot to pack, nor was there much else to be done. The formality of handing over the group at a parade with full military ceremonial appeared to be unnecessary and was probably also unwished for. The message they sent up to me with routine informality from the telex room was laconic: "Oberst Steinhoff, Johannes, to hand over Fighter Group 7 to Major W. with immediate effect. Further duties to be determined in due course. Signed, Head of Personnel." The order said neither where I should report nor whom I now came under. All it told me was: "Beat it, at the double—we don't need you any more."

What surprised me was that I felt no pain—only injured pride at being simply slung out like that. Nor did I feel as sad as when I had handed over Group 77, which I had commanded for years; then it had been like leaving a family. Fighter Group 7 was only eight weeks old, after all. The men who made it up had not had time to become a community; we had not yet started flying missions against the bombers. I knew I should be taking Rieber, who had been my batman since the Caucasus. Possibly I could also keep Fährmann, who had been my "Kaczmarek"* since Italy and was now my adjutant. But would they even let me fly anymore?

Lützow had announced his arrival, and when he arrived toward evening he said he wanted to stay the night. Rieber put up another camp bed in my room and retired to the kitchen to make supper.

Lützow and I sat in the vestibule of the summerhouse, which served as our lounge. The room was half dark, and we drank French cognac and beer in silence. I had pushed the telex across the table and he had read it and passed it back without a word. After about an hour we were joined by Fährmann and Klinpel, my "personal staff," good friends I had brought with me from the old group. My things—the battered leather suitcase that had flown with me to the farthest limits of the Pan-German Reich (it fitted exactly behind the cockpit shield of the Me 109) and the strongbox that also showed signs of having led a roving existence—stood by the wall, ready for the *n*th move.

Lützow poured himself another cognac and began: "The situation is indeed serious, gentlemen. The Reichsmarschall either has great plans for your commander—or he's retiring him. Yes, that'll be it— he'll pension him off and give him one of those state domains or should I say knightly estates for Knight's Crosses that lie in the fertile plains at the foot of the Caucasus Mountains. . . . The trouble is, nobody's told him the Russians have nearly reached Karinhall."†

He's cynical today, I thought; always when he's depressed he gets cynical and says things that would be enough to put him behind bars immediately; then he tanks himself up and gets the horrors.

Soon after this a jeep pulled up outside with the technical officer and the intelligence officer. They stamped the snow off their boots in the hall and came in, pausing in the doorway to raise their right arms in a casual salute.

Rieber brought the food. It was the usual menu of the last two

---

*Luftwaffe slang for the pilot who flew next to the leader of a formation (*J.S.*).

†Göring's own sumptuous mansion and estate on the Schorfheide, north of Berlin (*Tr.*).

years—"old man" (we called it "Alter Mann" from the initials AM for *Amministrazione Militare;* it was tinned meat of which we had brought a plentiful supply as booty from Italy) and scrambled egg. Night had fallen, and since the power supply was always slightly problematical in Brandenburg we had a number of lighted candles in empty wine bottles on the table—"just in case."

"Were you ever at Karinhall yourself, sir?" someone asked Lützow.

"Several times," he answered. "It was on my last visit there that I learned how to eat asparagus. . . . We sat at a long table with the Reichsmarschall at the head. He was wearing a leather waistcoat and a white shirt with puff sleeves and an open neck. He was really in his element, and you had to be damned careful not to come out with anything unsportsmanlike. There was a whole museum of stuffed heads staring down at us from the walls—all the unfortunate elks and royal stags of Rominten Heath that had made the mistake of lingering in the great hunter's sights. Suddenly there was a huge pile of fresh asparagus on the plate in front of me, giving off a mouth-watering aroma. I squinted across to my neighbor for a line on how to tackle this delicacy, but he was no help. In fact he seemed to be trying to conceal his own shakiness on the subject of court table manners by prolonging a conversation across the table long enough to pick up a hint from someone else. So I summoned up courage, reached gingerly for a shoot, and was just getting it balanced on my fork when the booming laughter of my host made me freeze. 'The man can't even eat asparagus,' he gurgled. 'Here—watch.' And with a hand as chubby and dimpled as a baby's he seized two asparagus shoots, wrapped his fingers round them, and raised them to his mouth. Quick as a flash, I did the same. Court table manners, you see."

"What was that about the knight's estates in the Caucasus—were they really serious about that?"

"They seem to have been," Lützow replied. "A fief from the Reich for everyone who got the Knight's Cross—a feudal benefice. But then an inflation of Knight's Crosses set in and prices went up—you had to have the Oak Leaves as well. Now there's nothing left to grant, and the Oak Leaves—or rather their bearers—are withering as fast as the Reich. The problem will solve itself in the end."

The room was full of tobacco smoke and the smell of men. Rieber came in with more bottles and put them on the table. Just then the telephone rang. Major Erich Hohagen, the commander of the Brandenburg wing who lived somewhere in the forest on the other side of the airfield, wanted a word with me.

"*Herr Oberst*, I hear that as of today you are no longer our commander. They tell me you first heard of it when you got back today—I mean that you had been dismissed overnight. This makes me extremely angry."

"Thank you," I said, "very kind of you, but it's not worth getting worked up about—they must have their reasons."

"Sir," Hohagen went on after a pause, "I have not been in this group for very long, but it's my opinion that this is no way to treat an officer—let alone a group commander. May I ask where they are transferring you?"

"According to the telex they're not transferring me anywhere for the moment."

After a further silence he said in an exaggeratedly loud voice: "I beg to report, sir, that I shall be leaving here with you. I am having terrible headaches again—my wound, you know—and I have sent for the medical officer." Then, dropping his voice to an urgent whisper, he went on: "Before he comes I propose to wreck the place. I can prove I am not accountable for my actions because of my injury."

He paused again, evidently exhausted. He'll do it, I thought to myself; if I know Erich Hohagen he'll do it. I had come across few men more straightforward in word and deed. He would reduce the place to matchwood without thinking twice about it.

I remembered the first time I had seen him. He was standing in the dim light of the single lamp that scantily lit the ticket hall of Augsburg station when I arrived for my conversion training to the Me 262 at Lechfeld airfield. He wore a black cap of the kind students wear after a bad duel, and it was pulled right down over his eyes, though some of the straw-colored hair still escaped. In defiance of every dress regulation (which we fighter pilots had in any case stopped observing long before) he had wound a fox fur round the collar of his yellow leather jacket (British booty—Dunkirk, probably). And he wore fur boots. The only "regulation" parts of his rig were the bit of trouser leg visible (Luftwaffe blue) and the Knight's Cross pinned to the fox fur. His injury was from when he had had to crash-land his Focke-Wulf after a dogfight—a belly-landing in a field that was much too small for the purpose. Airscrew and engine had buried themselves in a bank and he had smashed his skull on the reflex gun sight that stuck up slightly

in the cockpit. The surgeon had replaced part of his skull with a piece
of plastic and skillfully pulled the skin together over the disfigure-
ment. Even so the once virile, regular features had gotten out of balance. The two halves of his face no longer quite matched.

"What are your plans, sir?" The voice at the other end of the line
spoke up again.

"Man, I wish I knew. Lützow's here—they'll be starting on the
official farewell speeches soon. . . ."

Silence again. Then, clearing his throat, he went on in that charac-
teristic manner of speaking he had: "I should like to be there, sir—
request permission to join you later. However, as I am in the process
of inebriating myself I should like to apologize in advance in case I
should step out of line at all. . . ." There was another pause, during
which I was aware of his breathing. He cleared his throat again.
"*Herr Oberst*, I have made another important decision. I shall no
longer be wearing my Knight's Cross—in fact I've taken it off already."

I was so dumbfounded I said nothing for several seconds. Then,
recovering myself: "But that's absurd! It's no skin off your nose what
they do to me. . . ."

"Oh indeed it is—very much so. I have always been in full agreement with your critical remarks about Fatty and his clique. You have
been fearlessly frank. Now they sling you out. Well, I shall go with
you!" And with that he hung up.

I had no means of knowing it then, but Major Hohagen was, as a
member of the "mutineers' unit" toward the end of the war, to be one
of the last who were still taking off to fight the bombers at a time
when the Reich no longer existed.

I came back to find the room full of people. It stank like a pub.
The beer bottles stood on the table in serried ranks. Lützow was half-
lying in a chair, drawing figures with his index finger in a pool of
schnapps on the wooden tabletop.

"Hohagen's just smashing up his billet—says he's *non compos
mentis*."

"He is, too," said Lützow. "How can they let a man fly an aircraft
with a piece of plexiglass instead of a skull. . . ."

"He's renounced his Knight's Cross as well," I added.

"The gesture shows character," Lützow conceded, "but it's far too
late for that kind of thing to have any effect—even if we all did it."

The babble of voices and laughter was louder now. Suddenly I felt so wretched I could have wept. All these men knew that they now had a new commander and that I was expected to disappear from the scene. But did they care? Apparently not. Apparently they too saw it as just another sign of the decay that was steadily eating away at the Reich and the Wehrmacht. Göring had considered putting together a company of "out-of-work" generals. In his desperate search for sweeping excuses his mistrust of his officers had become almost pathological, leading him to wholesale disparagement of the entire officer corps ("Cheats and frauds! They're cowardly, they shirk their responsibilities . . ."). Anyone who had heard us that night, talking so cynically and so self-destructively, anyone who had seen that dissolution of everything that went by the name of military discipline, unconditional obedience, or Prussian correctness, would have heartily agreed with Göring that we were just a "bunch of dead-beat gypsies."

We had been warned to stop being so free with our criticisms. The home front was firmly in the grip of the party machine, which sniffed defeatism as soon as anyone expressed the slightest doubt about victory and made short work of silencing him. That night, however, all the barriers of soldierly discipline were down. Göring was referred to insolently as "Fatty" by one and all, Hitler was the "Gröfaz" (our scurrilous version of *grösster Feldherr aller Zeiten*, the "greatest military commander of all time"), the party high-ups were the "golden pheasants." The fellows were making an ungodly din, swapping jokes that were anything but respectable, and drinking to excess. Meanwhile my (former) staff pilots and the non-flying officers had turned up. They all sensed that this was "the end," that the collapse was near, and because they were incapable of imagining what lay beyond the catastrophe they showed in their helplessness that side of themselves that found expression in cynicism, swaggering, and disrespect. The war having taught them not to think further than the next morning, they blinded themselves to the inevitable and manifested an indifference that in some cases was even genuine.

"You know my father has given up his evening broadcasts?" Lützow asked me quietly. (Ever since 1940 Admiral Lützow had at short intervals given a commentary of German radio on the situation at sea.)

"Yes, I'd noticed. Why—because there's nothing but bad news anymore?"

"He's so bitter and pessimistic I'm frightened for him. They asked him to carry on and inspire confidence with his clear, unemotional reports on the naval situation. But he told them he wasn't prepared under any circumstances to describe how an exhausted U-boat arm was being wiped out crew by crew as a result of neglect of the fundamental principles of strategy and good sense."

"Have you talked to him about the hopeless situation we're in?"

"Many times, Macky. But it was only after that commanders' meeting at Gatow—the one before the 'Areopagus'—that I first told him we'd had all we could take and that in my opinion we should do something. It was as if I'd come out with something utterly monstrous—something I shouldn't even have thought, let alone said. Don't forget he belongs to a generation that still suffers from the trauma of the sailors' mutiny. He's never got over the defeat of 1918. When I cried on his shoulder about the way Fatty had been treating us and how he had cold-bloodedly ignored the fact that Udet and his CGS had committed suicide, he was appalled."

"Actually it's perfectly consistent, what Fatty's just done," I mused. "Why should I be upset? Why should I take it as an insult? He told us at that meeting in no uncertain terms—he wants loyal robots that will shoot down enemy aircraft to order. If a fighter pilot comes back from an operation alive, in Göring's book he's logically a coward!"

Lützow said: "I remember telling you after that disgraceful occasion—'Fatty's got to go!' I stand by that."

It had been early October 1944.

The group, wing, and squadron commanders of the Luftwaffe were gathered in the great hall of the *Reichsluftschutzschule* (I had not even known there was an "Imperial Air Defense School") in Gatow. The Reichsmarschall had ordered all unit commanders to attend who could anyhow be spared from the front as he wished to address them on the state of the Reich. The front being not so far afield now—for us day fighters of what was called "Reich Defense" it was right on our doorstep—the assembled company included practically all those who had so far survived this murderous war. If you excepted the front row it was a young crowd—hardly a man over thirty. The front row comprised the generals, men in the prime of life, some of them even with thinning hair; unlike us they wore decorations from the First World War as well.

The hall was filled to the last seat with the men who in this fifth year of the war led the Luftwaffe's flying units. One was struck by how much younger the fighting generation had become. The fantastic losses suffered in the big battles and at the major turning-points of the war had meant a continual moving-up to fill the place of the man in front. The result was that officers who had only passed out during the war now commanded groups. But also former NCOs, experienced veterans of hundreds of battles, had become officers and were now in command of the units they had risen in. There, too, sat the young, highly decorated officers whose faces every German knew from the illustrated magazines and the picture-postcard stands. In the front row sat the General of Bomber Pilots, young, slim, with a narrow, fine-featured face. The General of Fighter Pilots beside him, moustached and virile, made a striking contrast.

"I wonder what he's got in store for us today," said Lutzow, who was sitting on my right. "More abuse, I'm afraid—he turns it out without thinking now."

"Yes," I said, "he's slowly becoming a menace with his everlasting tongue-lashings. I can't stand the sight of the capon!"

At that moment the "capon" entered the hall. We leapt up amid a noise of scraping chairs. The senior general, commander of the "Reich" Air Fleet, was on his feet in front of the giant with his hand raised in the German salute. "*Herr Reichsmarschall,* beg to report . . ." We're being modest today, I noticed; only the pilot's badge set with diamonds adorned the massive breast. Standard black boots, white general's piping on the breeches, no Grand Cross.

What followed I shall never forget.

Without wasting any time on preliminaries he launched straight into a corrosive diatribe, heaping the most humiliating reproaches on the heads of us fighter pilots. The situation was critical, he said, and the German people wanted to know why its fighter pilots were such a craven failure. Formation upon formation of Flying Fortresses went about their work of destruction in a clear blue sky—and not a single German fighter to be seen. "I've spoiled you," he shouted. "I've given you too many decorations. They've made you fat and lazy. All that about the planes you'd shot down was just one big lie. Do you think anybody believes those astronomical figures? A pack of lies, I tell you!

We've made the most almighty fools of ourselves in the eyes of the British. You didn't make a fraction of the kills you reported."

On and on he raved, completely out of control. I felt deeply ashamed. How could he do it in front of the bomber, reconnaissance, and transport pilots? What was he after? Did he really think his cynical indictment was going to fan our fighting spirit and fill us with fresh dedication? During the brief pauses in his tirade you could have heard a pin drop in that great hall. Most of his listeners were staring at the floor between their feet, trying to hide their feelings behind masks of indifference. Suddenly I noticed the microphones on the speaker's desk. Cables ran from there into a cabin in which technicians were busy behind soundproof glass. The whole thing was being recorded! The whole nauseating rant about our cowardice and depravity was being engraved on gramophone records! (What is more, the records were subsequently sent out to all units.)

As far as the vulgar jibes went there was nothing in the whole theatrical performance that was not already familiar to me. But for sheer cynicism and arrogance he outdid himself on this occasion, pointing a quivering forefinger at us in front of all his other pilots and calling us cowards, liars, and malingerers. Eventually he calmed down a little, and there followed a few glib phrases: ". . . I'm not saying they're all cowards . . . but there's many a sergeant who's an example to his officers." It was the officers, of course, with their special rights and privileges, that bore the brunt of his contempt. Then at last it was over and he stamped sweating from the podium.

On his feet immediately, the senior general began in a loud, throaty voice: "*Herr Reichsmarschall*, in this hour of darkness we are filled with a thrilling determination to persevere until victory is ours. We have taken your earnest words very much to heart, sir, and we pledge unreservedly the last drop of our blood in the fight for Führer and Reich."

I glanced across at Lützow. Tears were running down his cheeks.

"We pledge unreservedly . . ."—how dare he? By what right did he presume to speak in our name? "Filled with a thrilling determination . . ."—the stocky little grey-haired general sits in his bunker surrounded by his staff and sends units into combat the way you move flags on a map. Instead of making a stand for us fighter pilots he starts spouting this pompous rubbish.

As Lützow and I drove back to his place together he slowly, hesitantly began to talk:

"I'm disgusted with myself, Macky—disgusted! Why didn't I have the guts to rip off my Knight's Cross and hurl it at his feet?"

"Why didn't I for that matter, Franzl?" I said. "But what good would it have done? He despises us. We're his scapegoat—it's we who have to answer for his walloping mistakes."

"No—today we should have done something. We owe it to all the fellows who in spite of everything climb into their aircraft every day and take off and fight. I'm ashamed."

We drove in silence along the shore of the Havel. It was a beautiful late-autumn day; the leaves of the breeches and sycamores glowed red in the sun.

"We've got to do something, Macky. We make ourselves accomplices if we just look on while these bunglers let the Reich be reduced to ashes and rubble. One thing at least is certain now—Fatty's got to go!"

It was long past midnight when Rieber called me to the telephone again. The medical officer informed me—as if it had been the most natural thing in the world—that Major Hohagen had demolished the contents of his flat, torn off his Knight's Cross, and was talking confused nonsense. "He needs immediate psychiatric treatment. He's unfit for service. He started flying operations again much too soon after so serious an accident."

"I know, I know," I told him. "Report the matter to your new commander. It's none of my business anymore. . . ."

"But *Herr Oberst*, he's your friend—what shall I do with him?"

"Tell him to get over here and join the party."

Not long afterward a noisy crowd came bursting in, led by Hohagen—minus his Knight's Cross. Swarming round our table, they launched into the song *Auf Wiedersehen, auf Wiedersehen.* . . .

"Had you heard Woitik was killed yesterday?" Hohagen asked me when they had finished.

"Good God—was he still flying on probation, then?"

"Right! Hats off to him, too—he must have shot down six or seven Flying Fortresses single-handed, usually having to bale out himself because his plane had been hit. But he always made it back to his unit—back to his friends, the pariahs of the Luftwaffe who were on probation like himself."

"We tried everything to get his sentence repealed," Lützow put in. "We took his case right to the top—to the Reichsmarschall. We recommended he be taken off probation and awarded the Knight's Cross, but Göring refused to listen. Woitik had got married and we wanted his widow to have more than just a captain's provision if anything happened to him. But Fatty said no."

"But that's inhuman!" I protested. "His court toadies must have talked him into that one. They don't know the kind of fear a man has to fight down when he attacks a Flying Fortress. It was fear made Woitik drink."

Woitik had joined us at the Channel in 1940—the last of a series of commanding officers who had either been replaced because they were simply not up to the demands of that battle for England or because after a few sorties they had failed to come back. Everyone knew his background: freestyle wrestling champion of Westphalia, a successful Spanish Civil War, which had seen him promoted from the ranks; good-natured, a heavy drinker, no good with women.

I had last seen him in a hunting lodge east of Smolensk little more than a year later. We had retreated in disorder from Klin, an airfield not fifty kilometers from the outskirts of Moscow. We had six aircraft left, and they were earthbound—even supposing we could have taken off in that snow—because we had no parts and no fuel. Useless in the air, the wing had been detailed for infantry duty. Woitik had ordered me to make my own way to the headquarters of the General of Fighter Pilots in East Prussia to protest at this "demotion" and get us withdrawn for reorganization instead, but when I looked in to report my departure my commanding officer was too drunk to hear what I was saying.

After that he went downhill fast. Warned by telephone one night that the Russians had broken through, he failed to take appropriate action and as a result several pilots and ground-staff personnel were killed. Woitik was court-martialed, degraded, and assigned on probation to a fighter squadron engaged in "Reich Defense." There, although he had not seen action for months—he had virtually given up flying himself—he started pulling down one Flying Fortress after another. Not that he had given up drinking. He drank against fear. They said the first thing he did when he landed to refuel was to take a good slug from the bottle. But before long he had shot down more of the big bombers single-handed than anyone else and by any normal standards he should have been decorated for it—and highly. If this was probation, he had proved himself beyond a shadow of doubt. The Reichsmarschall, however, thought otherwise, and Woitik was still on probation when they buried him.

The noise dropped toward morning. Some of us gathered round while the faithful Rieber brought hot coffee and fried eggs. Others were asleep in their chairs, mouths hanging open, and at one table they were still talking and gesticulating vigorously. There was a general "morning after" feeling and I was at a low ebb.

Suddenly one of the men at the table where the lively discussion was in progress jumped up and strode across to where the big picture of Göring hung on the wall (military pose, loose grey cloak, gold-embroidered cap and marshal's baton clasped before the belly in a gorgeously beringed hand). He carefully took it down from its hook, carried it over to the window, and with a powerful swing of his arm hurled the Reichsmarschall through the glass. Everyone sat up with a start at the crash—and stared wide-eyed at the empty wall.

"Time I disappeared," whispered Lützow, gripping my arm.

Rieber had spotted the signal and quickly took Lützow's things out to the car. Lützow followed him.

"Franzl, I'll be coming over in the next few days," I called out to his retreating back.

3

Gatow
December 1944–January 1945

It was in a mood of wretched depression that I collected together the last of my things the morning after my "dismissal." Rieber gave me a hand, and as coffee beans, ham, and bottles of vermouth found their way from the mess stores into my luggage he talked about the future. He did so in a subdued voice that made what he said sound like consolation. He had picked up so much "destructive defeatism" lately that he unhesitatingly identified himself with the defeatists.

"Don't let it get you down, sir. The whole bloody business will be over before long and you can . . . I'm packing the coffee for madam, look—she likes her cup of coffee. And here's a couple of pairs of silk stockings I picked up in Italy—just madam's size . . ." But then it got the better of him and he burst into recriminations about the callous way I had been slung out. "They could at least have given you the car for a few days, and the new bloke could have come over and said he was sorry. . . ."

"Forget it, Rieber," I said. "A lot worse things have happened in this war. When they don't need you anymore they kick you out and you're nothing, whether you've taken the rap or not."

"But you're not just anyone. What do they think they're doing, treating a Knight's Cross with Oak Leaves and Swords like that."

I had no answer to that one. I could not have cared less about my decorations than I did at that moment, having begun to hate the people who had awarded me them. What "they" thought they were doing was something I had not known for a long time, and to my surprise I did not even feel humiliated or hurt. Not in the least. What bothered me was the idea that, with the war sliding hopelessly toward catastrophe, I could not fly anymore, could not lead my group anymore. It was that which gave me a feeling of being "exposed," of floating on a raft in the middle of the ocean, utterly alone. As an officer without a command I was virtually nonexistent. It was as if I had been killed in action.

The only person I could have appealed to was the General of Fighter Pilots, who had recommended me for this posting two months before—but he had long been *persona non grata* himself and he knew there was no diverting destiny now. Nor was he the man to go to for consolation or for a shoulder to cry on. He was a tough soldier with no illusions, and at best he would have repeated the dry, brutal verdict he had delivered in a perfectly calm voice two days previously.

I had called on him at his office—I think it was to beg for a couple of aircraft or some component or other.

I knew in advance he would not be able to help. The organization of regular supplies had long since slipped from the general staff's grasp. The Reich was bleeding like a wounded deer, and planned production and orderly distribution were things of the distant past. And yet they had achieved the astonishing feat of producing a total of 40,600 aircraft during 1944, including 4,000 fighters—an enormous, indeed a gigantic figure compared with what we had been producing at the beginning of the war.

With the help of all those not fit for active military service—old or seriously wounded men, women of all ages, and the thousands of prisoners—the Messerschmitts and Focke-Wulfs had been assembled in makeshift factories, small workshops, road tunnels, and gravel pits up and down the country. But there was no one to fly them anymore, no one to wield these murderous weapons. The decimated groups no longer constituted combat-worthy formations. And there was barely enough fuel left to fly with—let alone to practice combat operations. So there they stood: row upon row of brand-new aircraft lined up on airfields, in forests and gravel pits, and along the roads, looking like wasps in their colorful camouflage paint—and no use to anyone anymore.

Galland had heard me out with an ill humor, answering only briefly as if to say: You know yourself I can't do anything for you. No one up there listens to me anymore anyway.

Then he turned to the map that covered the while of one wall. The shrinking Reich was represented with the aid of pins and little red flags in such a way that a series of concentrically diminishing lines focused on the capital. What was left was alarmingly little. Like the limits of arrogance the zigzag threads followed the Volga past Stalingrad, went up around Moscow, and descended the Atlantic coast to the Pyrenees—now thousands of kilometers from the pathetic remainder.

"We lost this war long ago," he said somberly. "God forgive us after all we've done to them."

I was grimly absorbed in sorting out my few possessions into light hand luggage to take with me and the remaining, heavy stuff including my winter outfit that I wanted to dump somewhere when Rieber called me to the phone: "Hauptmann K. would like a word with you, sir."

"That's it," K. said, straight out, "—the general will be removed from his post in the next few days. The new masters are already making their presence felt at Jagdwaffe headquarters. You've got to do something, sir."

Well, I was in the mood for "doing something." All of a sudden my attack of resignation was over. I no longer felt so utterly alone but was aware instead of how my suppressed feelings were transforming themselves into angry energy. I still had my friends—people who thought as I did. "I'll get on to Lützow immediately," I said. "Of course we must do something," and after a pause: "For the next few days you can contact me through Oberst Lützow. Take care, K."

It took no more than a few minutes to get Lützow on the phone. "I want to come over, Franzl. All hell's broken loose at Jagdwaffe headquarters. Since they've known the general's about to be dismissed they've become more and more shameless. I can be at your place in three hours. It may be for days, it may even be for weeks—no one wants to know about me anyway."

"Yes, do come right away. You can stay as long as you like."

As Rieber and I left the house where I had lived with the group staff, the cleaning women were just clearing up the remains of our nocturnal celebrations. Of my former staff officers not one turned up to see me off. Not that I felt like saying a lot of good-byes. I had only commanded the jet-fighter group for a little over two months. In fact the pilots were all strangers to me. They had flown no operations yet nor been involved in any action, and I had sensed that of the hot-headed eagerness to prove oneself in single combat that had led to the Jagdwaffe's great achievements in the first year of the war little or nothing was left.

Rieber had strapped up his bags and got ready to come along with me without a transfer order or anything. "We'll sort it out later," I said. We had always sorted it out later—when he had followed me from the Caucasus to Stalingrad, and then when he had gone on to Sicily with me, both times without any instructions from Personnel.

I was delighted to find Lützow in a mood that held no trace of pessimism or resignation. He was exhilarated at the prospect of doing something at last, and we plunged straight into a discussion of our plans.

It seemed to us advisable to keep the circle of those involved to a minimum and only take our closest friends into our confidence. Not many people were eligible for so dangerous an undertaking anyway—ultimately no more than a handful.

Hauptmann K. of Galland's staff reported that the situation at headquarters was close to anarchy. Although the general had not yet officially been removed from office, everyone knew that it was only a matter of days now. Meanwhile we made telephone calls, wrote coded letters, and arranged a meeting.

We met in Oberst Trautloft's hunting lodge on the edge of the Wannsee late one grey January afternoon. The sky was overcast, and snow made driving difficult and the roads treacherous. The lodge was only a few minutes from Galland's headquarters. It consisted of a single, square room, and when I opened the door a wave of warm air laden with cigar smoke washed over me.

We were four group commanders, the Director of Day Fighters, and Major Br. from Galland's staff. It had been a job to get Oberst Neumann up from Italy, but in the end we had managed to find him a seat in a bomber.

Lützow, barely recognizable in the semidarkness, asked for silence. He spoke clearly and with concentration. "Macky here and I thought it was time that the Jagdwaffe commanders who know and trust one another as friends got together to consider whether there is still a way out of the disaster. I want to try and sum up what has happened over the last few months, and then I want to ask the question whether we are not going to put ourselves in the wrong if we continue to look on without lifting a finger."

He spoke of the dilettantism of our air defense, of Göring's cynical recklessness, and of the infamy of putting the blame for the destruction of our cities on us. He mentioned the commanders' meeting in Gatow the previous October and the futile "Areopagus" of six weeks later. What had happened over the last few months we knew exactly. Even those from the Italian and Russian fronts who had followed events in the Reich with less sense of direct involvement fully grasped the hopelessness of the military situation.

"In the last few days," he went on, "we have had confirmation of the rumor that the General of Fighter Pilots was about to be removed from his post. But this is only the latest of a whole series of humiliations that we have so far—much too long, it seems to me—accepted without protest."

(When shortly before this we had told Galland of our plans he had expressed the wish that we should confer in his absence. "But please don't concern yourselves about me," he had said. "You must keep the cause you're taking up quite distinct from anything that may happen to me personally or in my capacity as General of Fighter Pilots.")

We had listened to Lützow in silence, drawing on our cigarettes or cigars, sipping our brandy, and staring straight ahead of us. Suddenly it was clear to us all that from now on every word counted, that we were possibly in the process of making decisions that would put us beyond the pale of loyalty.

Lützow spoke again: "Surely this inactivity, this resignation, coupled with our apparent readiness to take every insult lying down— surely this is simply to heap guilt on ourselves? Don't you see that the Areopagus was an indictment of us fighter pilots for political non-participation? Wasn't that the turning-point, at least as the Reichsmarschall saw it? That was when he dropped us for good. He promoted the general when he'd already chosen his successor. And he fell more and more for the latter's idea of fitting out the IXth Flying Corps,

General P.'s bombers, with the Me 262 to turn it into his 'vengeance corps.' A few more farcical ideas like that and this country's fate is sealed."

"Isn't it that already?" Neumann threw in. "I think we should ask ourselves whether there's still any point in doing anything. What good did the 20 July business do? The whole insurrection was a failure. Everyone who had anything to do with it they got rid of, and the disaster continued its course as before."

"I don't think," Lützow went on levelly, "that we can duck our responsibility as easily as that. We must get clear in our minds whether we really are to blame for the fact that our cities are helplessly exposed to bombardment. Göring after all never stops saying that 'the poor people only have to suffer because of the incompetence and cowardice of the Jagdwaffe.'"

"We are convinced that we can put a stop to this devastation from the air and save the lives of innocent people," I said.

"Right"—this was Trautloft—"then let's first of all try and establish whether we have made mistakes in the past and whether the general bears any blame."

"My considered opinion is that we, the 'famous German Luftwaffe,' were never equipped to fight a war of this kind," I answered. "There has been a great deal of frivolous irresponsibility right from the start. I don't want to talk about the political adventure we've all let ourselves in for. I'm simply criticizing the military dilettantism of Göring and his advisers. They have always favored an offensive war in the air but without equipping the Luftwaffe accordingly. They never had much time for air defense, and when they were forced to defend the Reich because the bombers were getting through to Berlin they did so in a dilatory and half-hearted fashion—and it was too late anyway. They only built up the night-fighter arm after the first catastrophic nighttime raids with no antiaircraft defense to speak of—think of Hamburg—had given them the fright of their lives. During the battle for England we couldn't escort the bombers to London and back and accept the challenge to combat because our flight duration was too short. The débâcle of 15 September 1940 was only possible because the Luftwaffe leadership's strategy was incoherent, shilly-shallying, and out of touch with reality and with the men who actually flew and fought. Our present fighter aircraft—the Me 262 excepted—are no longer equal to the demands of modern aerial combat, our successes in Africa and Russia notwithstanding. High command has changed its mind so many times during the course of the war— first a bomber offensive, then a 'fighter program,' then using the jets as *Blitz* bombers—that one can only talk of charlatanry. And now they lay it all at the door of those who throughout everything risked their lives without hesitation—among others, us!"

"But why didn't it occur to us to do something before?" asked Oberst Rödel. "Why didn't we rebel earlier and try and change things when there was still some hope of warding off catastrophe?"

"Quite clearly we young fliers are not to blame for starting this war," I went on. "Did we have any idea they were going to send us off to England and Norway and Africa and out to the Kalmuk Steppe? Hardly any of us were more than twenty-five at the time. No, the whole nation went along with the thing. So where were the men of years and experience who warned us against it?

"We have to admit that for those of us who were flying at the front the 20 July conspiracy came as an utter and complete surprise. Our horizon was of course limited because day after day our energies were wholly taken up by operations in our immediate section of the front— and that may be some excuse. But we blinkered ourselves too, and sometimes we really did live by the motto *'après nous le déluge.'* Our elders, the veterans of World War 1, were no help. With few exceptions they joined in, either enthusiastically or at least without reluctance, not thinking of what it might lead to. And let's face it—we allowed ourselves to be corrupted by accepting their orders and decorations although we should have seen we were being callously misused.

"All right—no one's denying any of that. But does that mean we are to look on passively while the Reich is destroyed, letting the *Volkssturm* and the poor buggers in the infantry and tank divisions do all the fighting? When *they* can't take the senseless, callous bally-hoo about our 'final victory'—which they already suspect is going to be a crushing defeat—when they can't take it anymore and desert they get hanged or shot. But all we need is a chit from the medical officer and off we go for convalescence, or skiing in Zürs, or to the Fighter Pilots' Rest Home."

"That's just it," Lützow said decidedly, "—we have no right to be the prima donnas of this war, picking out all the plums and going on leave whenever we get a bit fed up."

"Which brings us back to the point," I said. "Quite obviously no 'miracle weapons' are going to win this war anymore. But with proper use of our resources we can ward off a good deal of mischief— buy time, maybe put a stop to the daylight raids completely for a bit. . . ."

"Buy time," Neumann broke in bitterly. "Why, with the end already in sight?"

"Because we cannot stand around doing nothing while criminals drag the country to ruin. And because there is also such a thing as being answerable to history," said Oberst von Maltzan.

We were silent then, realizing that now there was no turning back. Maltzan had had to face the question of conflicting loyalties earlier than the rest of us—when relatives of his were arrested after the 20 July plot. As my *Jagdfliegerführer* in Italy he had shared his bitterness with me on many an evening, telling me then that he had long since lost faith in a positive outcome to the war, let alone in victory.

It was Maltzan again who broke the silence: "Giving up and sloping off to the Fighter Pilots' Rest Home to sulk would be irresponsible. We must have the courage of our convictions and act. The question is, what do we do?"

"Fatty's got to go," came Lützow's stock answer. "He's got to go and his whole clique with him. What we need to do is discuss ways and means of getting rid of him."

"The surest way of getting rid of him is of course to shoot him," offered Major Br. Although for a moment we were shaken rigid by this monstrous proposal, there were traces of amusement on the faces around the room. Br. had something of a reputation as a revolutionary and was in the habit of expressing his contempt for the "non-effectives" in the Luftwaffe high command with searing irony whenever he was given the chance. Miraculously he had always got away with it, although he was unsparing in his criticism of Hitler as well.

"That would admittedly be logical but it would not solve the problem," said Trautloft. "What's the good of shooting him if Luftwaffe strategy remains unchanged? Fatty must be forced to give up his command—he can be shunted off into some sinecure where he can do no more harm. In his place we must have someone competent who will ensure that the air defense of the Reich is planned and executed in the way we think right."

"It wouldn't be all that easy to shoot him, either," put in Maltzan.

"He's taken such a dislike to making troop visits nowadays that no one can say with any certainty when and where he's going to turn up. And to get to speak to him personally at the Air Ministry or at Karinhall we'd first have to negotiate the various 'official channels'—all of whom would ask us: 'What do you want to see the Reichsmarschall for?' And if we did penetrate that far we'd be subjected to the same undignified search as when you go and get a medal from Hitler."

I could in fact have shot him myself—coolly, calmly, and with no risk of anyone trying to stop me—only three months before this. But it had not even occurred to me to do so; I was not yet desperate enough at the time.

It was at Schönwalde, where we had just arrived with the three wings of Fighter Group 77 as part of the reserve that the General of Fighter Pilots was building up for the "decisive blow." I was busy—after the years of front-hopping—getting used to the drab realities of life in the Reich and preparing myself and my pilots for the tough prospect of defensive operations against the Flying Fortresses, when Göring suddenly announced a visit.

It was raining on the day, so the pilots formed up in one of the bigger hangars with the doors wide open to await the Reichsmarschall's arrival. They were a fine body of young men, though the number of those with veteran combat experience I could have counted on the fingers of one hand.

As the convoy of vehicles drew up on the apron outside the hangar I gave the order: "Attention! Report to the Reichsmarschall—eyes right!" and walked over to his big Mercedes. It took him a while to squeeze himself out of the car. Then, having been helped into his winter coat—superb fur lining, magnificent opossum collar—he grasped the marshal's baton and stood to attention.

"*Heil Hitler,*" he trumpeted in his powerful, high-pitched voice. No "Gentlemen!" no "Soldiers!"—just a laconic "*Heil Hitler!*"

"*Heil Hitler, Herr Reichsmarschall!*"

Immediately he strode over to the right wing of the formation and began his inspection. I introduced the wing commanders. He gave each a perfunctory handshake, asked no questions, but went stomping off down the lines of pilots, jerking his baton up and down in front of his stomach by way of a salute. It struck me that he was nervous and insecure. Only once did he come to a halt—in front of

Leutnant Angerer, whom he scrutinized closely for a moment. Then, as if he had been searching for words, he suddenly burst out:

"Could you today, in this weather, fly deep into enemy territory—say into France or Belgium—attack aircraft with your cannon, and fly back here again?"

Why of all people does he have to pick on Angerer, I groaned inwardly; why couldn't he have asked Köhler, or Riedmeyer, or Säckel? Poor Angerer—the only reason why he had a squadron was that he was older than the bulk of the other pilots. His brain worked with the sluggish rhythm of a Lower-Bavarian peasant lad's and he spoke with the thick accent of his native hills—in, to make matters worse, a high-pitched, squeaky voice that sounded as if it had yet to break.

Angerer looked scared to death. He shifted uneasily, stood to attention again, and threw me an imploring look. "*Herr Reichsmarschall,*" he began elaborately. Then, peering out into the rain: "I could fly all right . . ."—another pause, during which the Reichsmarschall started to show signs of impatience— ". . . but I wouldn't be too happy about the—" (and here he used our slang word for navigation).

This time it was Göring's turn to cast an inquiring look in my direction. Then, however, he seemed to twig Angerer's problem. "Ah, yes," he said quickly, "—so you could fly. That's good. For the other thing you have these gadgets in your aircraft, don't you?"

I think every eye in that hangar must have blinked in disbelief. Highly sophisticated pieces of radio and navigational technology had just been referred to by Göring as "gadgets"—the word people used who understood nothing of such things. News of this testimony to the Reichsmarschall's technical "grasp" spread like wildfire through the whole Luftwaffe. "Gadgets"! And the man was our supreme commander!

His visit had the advantage of being brief. He appeared to have no further interest in questions concerning operations or the problems of the unit but wanted to push on to the next wing of the group as quickly as possible. All of a sudden I found myself sitting on the folding seat behind the driver of his great Mercedes, accompanying the Reichsmarschall on his tour of inspection.

We drove at a leisurely speed, and while the two gentlemen in the backseat enjoyed a merry chat—he had brought Bruno Loerzer along with him, an old friend and comrade from the First World War—I had plenty of time to observe them. It was not that they were unfriendly; they simply took no more notice of me than one does of the person one happens to sit opposite on the train.

The road led through a stretch of forest with a magnificent stand of old pines. Air mines had wrought a good deal of havoc here and huge trunks lay all over the place, their rootstocks, ripped from the ground with the earth still on them, reaching dead fingers to the sky.

The two gentlemen broodingly contemplated this scene of devastation. Then the Reichsmarschall cleared his throat and said: "It's absolutely scandalous, what these barbarians have done to the German forest! It will take years to make good this damage."

Lützow was talking again.

"No—we should put our case to Hitler. We must tell him right out that we believe the war to be lost. But at the same time we must rid ourselves of the burden of guilt involved in passively looking on while the Allied bombers terrorize the Reich—although we are convinced that a vigorous and workmanlike air-defense operation could save the lives of thousands of people. So we put it to him: Göring must be dismissed. If we fail to persuade him, at least we shall have eased our consciences and come out with what we feel to be wrong, dangerous, and irresponsible about the way the Luftwaffe is being led."

"Which is exactly what we'll all be shot for!" bellowed Major Br. from his corner. "Don't you fellows know the Führer is infallible?"

Night had fallen by this time. The air in the little room was becoming unbearable, and cognac and red wine were beginning to have their effect. It was not without some difficulty that Lützow managed to regain the floor. "Look—our problem isn't so insoluble," he said. "All we've got to do is consider the few alternatives still open to us and choose one. The suggestion that we get rid of Fatty by shooting him appears to have found no supporters. We're left with the possibility of seeing the Führer, telling him what's on our minds, and asking him to replace the Reichsmarschall as supreme commander of the Luftwaffe. But how do we get to see the Führer? Using official channels we'll never get past our immediate superior, who'll be very curious to know what we want with Hitler."

"OK—we try and convince Hitler to drop Göring," Br. chimed in again, supporting Lützow now. "Well, there's one way we can be dead sure of reaching him—we tell the SS about the situation and ask them to organize an interview."

"Right—Hitler will be able to change everything," said Lützow. "That's certain. There's one danger, though. Since he appointed Himmler supreme commander of the Home Guard the latter has become more power-hungry than ever. We might suddenly wake up and find ourselves in an SS Luftwaffe, and I don't imagine any of you want that. If flying weren't so difficult and didn't call for so much training and experience Himmler would have made a bid for us long ago!"

"The whole thing sounds damned dangerous," Trautloft warned. "Here's Himmler toying anyway with the idea of swallowing the Wehrmacht lock, stock, and barrel. And on the other hand the SS might take our suggestion the wrong way—and we all know what that would mean."

The discussion revived and there was some vehement opposition to taking the SS into our confidence. Then Br. spoke up again:

"I know an SS officer—Obergruppenführer O. He's often up at Oberjochberg with the bomber pilots so he knows something about Luftwaffe matters. Why don't we try via him?"

The meeting reluctantly agreed to send a reconnaissance party to talk to O. and find out whether we could get to Hitler through him.

"But supposing it misfires? Supposing he blabs to Göring?"

"You needn't worry about that—Himmler can't stand Fatty. There's much more danger of his trying to exploit the occasion to take over what's left of the Luftwaffe himself."

"And what if your attempt is unsuccessful?" Trautloft wanted to know.

"Then the only way will be to go to the senior fighter pilot in the Luftwaffe, Generaloberst Ritter von Greim, and ask him to take the matter up—if necessary with an official report to the Führer."

"And if he refuses?"

It was growing late. The discussion had tired us all and the apparent hopelessness of our undertaking depressed us. There was no more room for cynical cracks and macabre humour.

"We ought to get the general here," someone said.

Galland sat silent for a long time after Lützow had finished his résumé of our plans. Then—clearly, objectively—he began to speak about the past. Once again he passed the mistakes made by Göring and his staff soberly under review, and when he had done that he turned to the decline of the Jagdwaffe during the three years in which he had been General of Fighter Pilots. The fact that fighter units had not been set up as soon as it was realized that the heavy bombers were beginning systematically to destroy the Reich's capacity for survival had been his fault as well, he told us. He touched briefly on the tragedy of the Me 262 and on the powerlessness of the night fighters in the face of inadequate organization and means. Then, however, his control cracking, he burst into bitter complaints of the leadership's incompetence to recognize that the defense of the Reich only stood a chance if they concentrated their forces and gave up the ludicrous idea of recovering the offensive in the air.

He shuddered at the thought of the intrigues and libels that his opponents were using to get him out of the way. He realized that as far as his dismissal was concerned the die was cast. The bomb terror too would take its course and continue to wipe out our cities one by one and kill thousands of innocent people. Nevertheless it was his belief that the enemy air offensive could still be checked if two or three fighter groups were given the Me 262 and all experienced fighter pilots were concentrated in those units. Fitting out bomber groups with the Me 262 he described as irresponsible madness.

Then, putting the question whether it was our duty to intervene, he answered in the affirmative. He did not conceal the fact that he was sceptical of our chances of success. "Let's assume Hitler goes along with your suggestion and drops Göring in favor of von Greim, who then brings in new men and new methods and reorganizes our air defense in the way we think necessary. By concentrating all our forces we could effectively oppose the continued destruction of our cities—of that I'm quite convinced. And the fact that we could thereby save thousands of lives justifies your going ahead with this thing. But as to whether it will make any difference to the outcome of the war, my answer is 'no.' The Reich, or rather what's left of it, is on its deathbed. Hitler and Göring criminally underestimated the efficiency and potency of the Anglo-Saxon war machine. And I don't believe any miracle weapon is going to change things now."

We nodded in agreement, pleased that he had not tried to dissuade us from our undertaking. We had known for a long time that victory was out of the question.

"But take care if you're going to the SS," he warned. "Himmler's hunger for power is insatiable. He's already shown interest in intervening in the jet-fighter program—if only organizationally at first. And his flirtation with the 'Natter'* is only the beginning. The biggest danger is of their playing you false. The bomber pilots have long been politicizing with certain SS officers up at Oberjochberg—along the lines that came out clearly at Göring's 'Areopagus.' Do you remember—'We profess and believe . . .'! There you have it in a nutshell. Pull out as soon as it looks as if the SS is not prepared to help us and try approaching von Greim instead—see if he can get Göring out. If that fails too you're left with what is probably the least effective but most honorable way of settling disputes: tell Fatty to his face! Not that it will do any good, but at least you'll sleep better afterward—if he lets you, that is! He can be a brute when he's roused. Well, let's take the risk together. He'll assume I'm the ringleader anyway, so I'm involved automatically."

*A vertical takeoff, manned rocket aircraft planned for use as an interceptor against the Allies' heavy bombers. Its first and only flight was unsuccessful, the aircraft crashing shortly after takeoff (J.S.).

From the diary of General Galland, 1945

The SS leadership poked its nose more and more into Luftwaffe affairs. It concerned itself with armament; it even concerned itself with operations. A new post was created: Special Commissioner for Jet Aircraft. Göring appointed General Kammhuber to fill it. Hitler refused to sign the order and instead appointed his own man in the person of General Kammler of the Waffen SS. . . . The result was that Kammhuber was in effect subordinate to the SS general. . . .

My successor entered into contact with the SS and got as far as Himmler himself. Himmler informed Hitler of my alleged unreliability. I soon became aware that all my telephones were being tapped and that the security service [SD] was taking a lively interest in me.

4

Berlin
4 January 1945

Our appointment with Obergruppenführer O. was on 4 January. We took the suburban train and walked the short distance from the station to his villa. It was one of dozens in that part of the city: whitewashed, dormer-windowed, and showing little trace of architectural imagination, it stood four-square on its little plot of land. There was no name beside the bell-push on the gate, but the number was the one Major Br. had been given over the phone so I hesitantly rang the bell.

There were three of us—Major Br., Hauptmann K., and myself. Major Br. was our "contact." "I know O.," he had told us, "—not a bad fellow. He's a man you can talk to. But if I might make a suggestion, *Herr Oberst*—go easy on the criticism of the Führer and the top brass in general, except of course as far as Göring is concerned. They don't take at all kindly to it." Well, that was no news to me, and I resolved on this occasion to stay cool and objective, concentrating on making out a cogent case to the effect that Göring must be removed from his post.

The garden gate opened automatically, and as we walked up the path to the house we saw a man in SS uniform standing in the doorway waiting for us.

"*Heil Hitler!*" he said, springing to attention. "This way, please—the Obergruppenführer is expecting you."

He showed us into a room at the end of the hall with windows overlooking the garden. More living-room than office, it was furnished in an undistinguished manner. There was a large and rather nasty oak bookcase against the long wall and arrayed behind its glass doors what looked like a complete collection of the literature of the Third Reich. At the same time the files scattered all over the place, on tables and shelves, a small electric stove bearing a white coffee pot (filthy, with brown streaks of dried coffee down the sides), and the typewriter on the massive baroque desk indicated that this was also a working room.

We shook hands, all yelling "*Heil Hitler!*" and Major Br. tried (unsuccessfully) to play on his SS connections with a cheery smile and a confidential "Here we are, then." It was not until the door was closed and we were seated opposite the two SS officers that I began to realize what we had let ourselves in for. The Obergruppenführer was a young man—certainly not yet forty—with a baby face and a smooth, pink complexion. The other officer was older and unlike his companion wore his black uniform buttoned up to the neck. O.'s lips were set in a barely perceptible ironic grin. He appeared to have no intention of opening the conversation but merely sat there looking at us, his pudgy face a mask.

I do not remember whether I began what I had to say cleverly and in a manner calculated to give the impression that we were serious and our cause of crucial importance. I do remember that I was soon involved in expounding the kind of defensive strategy against the heavy bombers that we felt should be adopted, and that little by little I abandoned my initially tight control over the tone of my indictment and began to speak of Göring's unbelievable incompetence, the brutality that emerged in his dealings with us, and the burden of guilt that he had thrust upon us.

I spoke with some passion, and the two officers listened with lively interest, though their faces betrayed not the slightest sign of emotion. When, however, I went as far as to clothe our intentions in the words "We want to save what we still can," their faces turned to stone. From the way in which I had expressed myself it was not hard for them to deduce my true attitude to "victory."

It was the Obergruppenführer who began the interrogation—and it was soon clear that that was what it was to be. Did we fighter pilots, he wanted to know, really believe that—even given systematic concentration of all forces—we were still in a position to deliver significant blows? Would it not be nearer the truth to say that the Jagdwaffe was a demoralized and undisciplined rabble—as everybody knew it was?

In my rising indignation at the fact that this libel was now evidently common property I asked sharply: "Where do you get that idea from?" No "*Herr Obergruppenführer*," no nothing—just my naked anger.

Whereupon he launched into the litany of our sins. Was it or was it not true that the Allied bombers came waltzing daily over the Reich while the Jagdwaffe, on the pretext of bad weather, never got off the ground? And was it or was it not true that we were guilty of gross extravagances—"in these difficult times"—to wit, immoderate indulgence in booty (cognac from France, vermouth from Italy)? And what about the black POWs as commodores' "boys," and the horses, and the women, and the champagne . . . ? The whole litany, as I said.

I listened in utter astonishment, my only thought being, "What business is that of his?" Then my eyes wandered to his left breast, where a not inconsiderable display of colorful decorations from Romania, Bulgaria, and Italy provided company for a Military Cross, first-class. An able fellow at any rate, I thought, even if he does seem to cultivate those abilities chiefly in the rear, well away from the shooting. But his affected Puritanism annoyed me and I retorted sharply that when all was said and done our job was to shoot down enemy aircraft and that that was what we were doing—granted, with limited success, but that was because of the circumstances I had just described.

The effect of this remark was to trigger off a crash course in National Socialism. Neither "circumstances" nor the alleged inferiority of our aircraft nor any inadequacy on the part of the Reichsmarschall were responsible for our lack of success; we failed because we were not permeated through and through with the values of National-Socialist ideology. Doubting victory and doubting the Führer's genius as we did, we could not help being a failure. "Furthermore," he pontificated, "the flying abilities of the fighter pilots are far inferior to those of the bomber pilots. The bomber pilots have a solid training behind them and are a disciplined force. The Reichsmarschall's plan to equip an entire flying corps, the IXth Corps, with the Me 262 is a logical and correct one, and when that corps goes into action it will bring the Anglo-Saxons to their knees."

My companions were clearly scared to death at the turn the interview had taken and started giving me imploring looks ("Pack it in—you're talking our heads into the noose!"). But I was not prepared to be lectured to by a professional purveyor of fanaticism and blind belief in victory about how we ought to be fighting the war in the air. I knew full well what he wanted to hear from me—and yet I simply could not bring myself to tell the lies that would have improved our position. With a few allusions to the superiority of the German race, the German people's fanatical will to victory, the genius of the Führer, and the National-Socialist soul I would have been sure of his goodwill at least. But I had been through all this once already—when Göring's abortive attempt to solve the problems of the war in the air through the medium of an "Areopagus" had degenerated into a National-Socialist bible class.

Calmly, objectively, I refuted his whole amateurish assessment of the state of our air defense. It was "five minutes to midnight," I told him, and he could not relieve us of our responsibility to "save what we still could."

Hearing these words again the Obergruppenführer leaned back in his chair, crossed his arms, and gave me a cynical look. "Now tell me just what you mean by 'five minutes to midnight' . . ." he said quietly. "—'five minutes to victory,' I take it?"

As I maintained an embarrassed silence he went on with coldly threatening intensity: "Here you are talking about 'five minutes to midnight' when the Führer has mobilized the nation in a way that is without parallel in history. We are bombarding the British Isles with the V-1 and V-2! And that's only the beginning of our retaliation. An entire flying corps, a picked body of pilots filled to a man with fanatical confidence in victory, stands ready to strike a crushing blow at the Allied bombers. And the Führer has weapons at his disposal of which you cannot begin to guess the efficacy. . . . You claim the fighters are doing their best and shooting down enemy aircraft, yet you admit in the same breath that their successes are meager. Of course they are—because unless a man believes firmly in victory he will never be successful. You fighter pilots are unpolitical. You're simply not National Socialists and never will be."

I was nonplussed. And because I was convinced that the man was one of those arrogant careerists who had ruthlessly elbowed their way onto the political bandwagon of the Third Reich without ever exposing themselves to the physical dangers of war, I was suddenly afraid. But the anger still seethed in me and made me ask: "What are they then, *Herr Obergruppenführer*, these miracle weapons?" I went on: "Don't you think it's high time the IXth Flying Corps went into action against the bombers before every city in the Reich has been flattened?"

He brushed my objections aside. "The new weapons are under the Führer's direct command. He will know when is the right time to use them. But let me tell you this: the V-1 and V-2 are only a foretaste of what is to come!" The scepticism he read in my face evidently stung him because he went on: "I know what you fighter pilots are after: you want to get your hands on the IXth Flying Corps yourselves and make havoc of it the way you daily make havoc of what little is left of the Jagdwaffe with your uncoordinated, incompetently led, skimpily trained pilots. The pilots of the IXth Corps are an élite, I tell you! They'll take off in any weather *and* fight *and* make kills."

"That's just nonsense," I said roundly. "I was in Brandenburg when the General of Bomber Pilots made his pathetic attempt to fly the Me 262 through cloud cover blind without ground support. His theory about being able to work out an attack mathematically in advance and then fly it on instruments just goes to show that he's never been in a dogfight and has no idea what aerial combat is like at eight thousand meters. Galland's discussed it with him countless times."

That was as far as I got. He dismissed my remarks with a wave of his hand, gave a sign to his companion, and said with noisy sarcasm, "Galland, Galland. You must think we're naive. Did you suppose we'd take every fantastic thing you chose to tell us on trust? We listen to the other side too, you know—we're taking care of your Galland."

The second SS officer had meanwhile opened a cupboard in the corner and was wiring up a record player, loudspeaker, and amplifier. At a nod from the Obergruppenführer he switched on, and after the needle had made a scratching sound for a few moments we suddenly heard, very loud: "Galland speaking . . ." The voice filled the room. "Speer . . ." another voice boomed in answer. "Galland, I wonder if I could have a word with you about the defense of the Ruhr District. I'm getting very worried . . ." At a further nod from the Obergruppenführer the needle was lifted from the record and the apparatus switched off. Silence fell like a dead weight.

"You see," said O. with malicious mock-friendliness, "we listen to both sides—and only then pass judgment."

Before we quite realized what was happening we were out on the pavement again. Mumbling something like "Thank you very much" and "We must be going now" and pausing only to turn in the doorway and raise our arms in the German salute, we had scuttled out of the house and down the gravel path to the gate in a state of mind bordering on panic.

They were monitoring Galland's telephone calls! It meant that they certainly had their eye on me too—and on Lützow. I cursed myself for not having realized that of course we were being shadowed; the "Areopagus" had been a clear enough warning.

That same evening Franzl and I decided to speed things up before we were silenced—as might happen at any moment. There was no telling which way the SS might jump now. The next step in the program we had adopted in the hunting lodge must be taken immediately.

You've heard what Churchill told the British parliament a few weeks ago—that the whole of East Prussia and parts of Pomerania and Silesia are to be given to the Poles. Seven, ten, possibly eleven million Germans are to be uprooted and resettled.

It's all pure theory. It's ludicrous. A figment of his imagination.

Hitler addressing his generals,
28 December 1944

5
Litzmannstadt*
13–14 January 1945

Dawn was breaking as my car pulled up on the apron of Gatow airfield. Franzl Lützow stood shivering beside his Messerschmitt Taifun.

"Bastard won't start."

"They're hell when they're cold."

The mechanics had been knocking themselves out. In their black overalls and clumsy rubber galoshes they stamped in the snow and blew into their cupped hands, their breath turning to milky wreaths on the morning air.

"If we can't get off soon it'll start to snow and we'll have to give up."

It was 13 January. After a disturbed night in the chilly guest barracks, with someone noisily entertaining a *Blitz* girl—as we called our female comrades-in-arms—on the other side of the thin partition wall, I had hardly touched my meager breakfast of "special pilots' rations": malt coffee, bread, margarine, and scrambled-egg powder.

Franzl and I had spent the evening before in the lounge of the officers' home discussing for the nth time how we would convince Gener-

*German name of Lodz, Poland *(Tr.)*.

aloberst von Greim (a) that he must suggest to Hitler that he get rid of the Reichsmarschall and (b) that we fighter pilots, systematically engaged, could still put a stop to the destruction of our cities. We had drunk half a bottle of the general's best cognac and it had had the effect of removing Franzl's last inhibitions, making him break out into regular tirades of loathing against the Reichsmarschall and picture to himself how different everything would be once Fatty was gone.

"Sometimes I think there's no point anymore," I put in. "What good will it do us, getting rid of Fatty?" The thing we were about to do was so monstrous that I was constantly plagued with doubts.

"The merest reminder of that capon's existence makes me sick. How could our generals ever let such a bungler wreck the Luftwaffe?"

"On the other hand you're right, of course," I said. "If our generals let us down, *we* can't just sit back and watch everything go to the dogs."

It was always the same old story—Franzl torn between loyalty and despair and bitterly holding forth against the bomb terror, calling it a "crime against humanity," and in the same breath muttering broken-voiced that "it serves us right" and "we've got a hell of a lot to answer for."

The first snowflakes were already blowing across the airfield when at last the Taifun fired. Flying round Berlin in a wide arc to the north, we picked up the railway line running east to Frankfurt-an-der-Oder and then negotiated low cloud and snow flurries across endless snow-covered wastes until we reached Litzmannstadt.

As the jeep taking us into town from the airfield threaded its way through the suburbs, snow was falling heavily and we could see nothing in front of us but a seething white wall of the stuff. Night had fallen and the masked headlights made driving pure guesswork.

We found von Greim's IIIrd Air Fleet headquarters in a state of nervous excitement. Housed in what was probably a school, it looked very much like every other staff headquarters I had seen in the East. Green oil paint covered the walls, and the corridors were dimly lit by weak lightbulbs hanging naked from the ceiling.

"Oberst Lützow and Oberst Steinhoff, acting on behalf of a group of Jagdwaffe officers, wish to speak to Generaloberst Ritter von Greim as the senior officer of the Jagdwaffe." That was how we had announced ourselves; he could have no idea of the purpose of our visit.

"Generaloberst von Greim will see you at about six," the orderly officer told us as he showed us to our rooms. "I'll fetch you in half an hour."

Von Greim was one of the old guard of Luftwaffe generals. A successful First World War career as a fighter pilot had earned him quick promotion, and since he had also been active politically he was regarded as solid and dependable. The virile, likable Bavarian positively radiated steadfastness. We used to call him "Papa Greim."

"Good evening, gentlemen. How was your flight?"

"No problems, *Herr Generaloberst.* We were able to land before the snowstorm got up."

The big, broad-shouldered man, his spectacles perched on the end of his nose, looked at us questioningly out of sea-blue eyes as if sensing that we brought bad news.

"Before we get down to business we must go in and hear the evening situation report—not that I expect you to enjoy the experience."

Laying an arm round both our shoulders, he led us along the corridor to the brightly lit sit. room. "Gentlemen," he told the assembled officers, "Oberst Lützow and Oberst Steinhoff will join us for this evening's session. Neither of them needs any introduction, I believe. Fire away, please, Mr. Kless."

The sit. table was a board several yards long laid on trestles. It very nearly filled the room. The large-scale map fixed to the board with drawing pins was adorned with crayon lines and colored flags symbolizing the eastern front from the Baltic to the Carpathians. Bright lamps with green shades were pulled down low, leaving the faces bent over the table from all sides in semidarkness. Section maps, tables of figures, and weather reports festooned the green-painted walls.

The staff officers looked pale and short of sleep. They had been on their feet since the early morning of the day before, harassed by one piece of bad news after another. The scene had an almost frightening quality. The white faces shone dully like ghosts in the gloom, while below them the uniforms with their decorations and the hands resting on the table were brightly lit. There was scarcely a movement.

We listened with growing attention to the general-staff officers' reports, following with our eyes the erratic course of the pointer as it slid along a front that no longer deserved the name. Wherever a broad red arrow on the map marked a breach the pointer would come to a halt and a dead silence would fall on the room as the speaker's matter-of-fact voice recounted the disaster.

There was no trace left of the detached, almost arrogant reeling off of facts and figures that had formerly characterized such sit. discussions, no more careless playing-down of the significance of "heavy defensive engagements," "tactical withdrawals," and "setting up a new rear position." The realization that this was something else altogether seemed to lie heavily on all present.

The long-expected major offensive from the Baranov bridgehead had begun. Two Soviet wedges, attacking in the early hours of 12 January, had driven themselves deeply into the German positions. A mere thirty-two divisions and eight armored corps took the brunt of this thrust against Krakow and central Poland, which the Soviets immediately followed up with an attack on the East Prussian front aimed at Ebenhausen, Schlossberg, Memel, and Tilsit.* The offensive appeared to have spread along the entire eastern front with the speed of a steppe fire.

The officers around the table were already familiar with the nuances of diction and phraseology used as soon as it was a question of defense and of our own forces. Their disillusionment was starkly evident as the speaker referred to "delaying tactics" and "curtailing the front." Catastrophes had been called that too often already.

Von Greim listened in silence, shaking his head disappointedly as he heard of his pilots being hampered by the weather, with the meteorologist unable to forecast any improvement. Meanwhile the telephone in the next room rang nonstop and orderly officers were coming in all the time to lay fresh reports on the table.

Only once did von Greim break his silence.

"Gentlemen, we expected this offensive, as you know, but we did not expect it to be so powerful. The question arises whether this represents the Soviets' final, all-out effort, as you have at times sought to persuade me. It may equally—and this is what I am inclined to think myself—be the beginning of the end. . . ."

I had followed the description of the débâcle with a beating heart.

*Now Slavst, Niman, Klaypeda, and Sovetsk *(Tr.)*.

It was almost as if I were being forced to visit all the stations of the failure and defeat of the Reich, with this sit. report adding the final word to a personal object lesson in the impotence and dilettantism of our military leaders. I had been through that frightful first Russian winter and seen the reckless, cold-blooded improvisation with which they had reacted to it. And because they failed completely to draw the moral of that appalling fiasco, in the following winter my fellow-pilots and I found ourselves in the Kalmuk Steppe, unable to land at the airfields around Stalingrad and obliged to look on helplessly while an entire army was left in the lurch. Then, that I might taste the cup of defeat to the full, they sent me off to North Africa, where the curtain had already gone up on the final act. The humiliating retreat up the Italian peninsula was followed by a brief guest appearance at the invasion of France, until finally, via northern Italy and Romania, my group was pulled back to the airfields around Berlin to participate in that hopeless battle against the bomber streams known as "Reich Defense."

A commanding officer who has taken an active part in the battles and defeats at the front, flying virtually every mission himself, is sometimes a sharper, more critical, and more accurate judge of the situation than the general-staff officer or commander who is physically far removed from it and has to rely on abstract information and maps. Particularly pilots, who actually see the extent of an offensive or an enemy breakthrough from the air several times a day, experience the course of an operation so immediately that they complain continually of the lack of vision of those who with their maps and their theoretical marching speeds of six to ten kilometers per hour are incapable of "thinking three-dimensionally."

I was becoming increasingly a prey to a state of anxiety bordering on despair. The Soviets were in East Prussia and on the frontiers of the Reich. The attempts to instill belief in various "miracle weapons" and in the great turning-point heralded by the approaching exhaustion of our enemies struck me as a transparent trick. I had commanded one of the "miracle weapons" myself—a whole group of jet fighters—and I knew only too well that the difference it made would not be decisive and that fate would take its course.

Anxious, discouraged, and filled with a deep disappointment, I thought of what had brought us here. We fighter pilots had started something we knew to be right and of vital importance, but we were too late. Too late because there was no more hope, because our words had been drowned in advance by the roar of this vast offensive, because no one was prepared anymore, at this late stage, to stick his neck out for something that would make no difference to our fate.

An anguished von Greim turned to the door. "Come on—I've heard enough."

We arranged ourselves round a fire of massive oak logs. An orderly placed a bottle of red wine on the table and left us alone.

"*Herr Generaloberst*," Franzl began, "we've come to see you as the senior pilots of the Jagdwaffe to tell you that we fighter pilots have lost faith in our leadership. Our confidence in the Reichsmarschall is now nil. We are aware that the Jagdwaffe has never recovered from the blood-letting it suffered during the battle for England. We are aware that crucial mistakes have been made and that it is too late to do anything about them. We still have a limited number of experienced, battle-tried fighter pilots. The younger pilots are under-trained and inexperienced; they don't survive more than a few sorties. We have been given a job that three years ago we would have rejected as a ridiculous impossibility: fighting heavily armed bombers and their escorts in every corner of the Reich. We have failed—we might as well admit it—to develop in time an ability to fly in any and every weather. But then when did we ever have time to do so, and where was the aircraft we could do it with? Much too late we have been given a new aircraft, a supersonic aircraft, the Me 262 jet fighter, but we've been given too few of them and it is, as I say, too late. The bulk of the new aircraft are going to bomber units, where we fail to see how they can be meaningfully employed.

"But none of this, sir, is the real reason why we fighter pilots have decided to take this step. The real reason is that we can no longer stand being forced to look on in a state of virtual inactivity while our cities are one after another bombed to dust. The Reichsmarschall refers to us publicly as cowards, abusing and slandering us constantly. Two years ago he called Galland a defeatist for saying he thought the four-engined bombers would soon reach Berlin. Today he makes us his whipping-boy for not having been able to stop them."

Von Greim, who had been staring stonily into the fire, shook his head at this point and Franzl broke off his philippic. For endless seconds no one said a word. The fire flickered dimly, the logs crackling and hissing.

Von Greim turned and looked first at Franzl and then at me with an expression that was strikingly bleak.

"And what do you propose to do about it?"

The question was so direct that for a moment I had trouble in answering.

"Air defense," I began, "and I don't mean flak but the day-fighter and night-fighter units—air defense has always been a bit of a stepchild with the Reichsmarschall and the CGS. It is our conviction that proper use of the Jagdwaffe—concentrated coordinated fighter action—could be made so effective as to put a stop to the systematic destruction of our cities and the terrorization of the German people. We did it at Schweinfurt and Nuremberg and we can do it again. The Reichsmarschall's getting the wrong advice, but his own ideas are just as farcical. Excuse my language but this is really what it's all about. We consider that to go on thinking offensively in this situation and keep bomber command at its present enormous strength makes no sense at all. In our opinion using the Me 262 primarily as a bomber is utterly wrong. Also we're fed up with the Reichsmarschall bawling us out. We want him dismissed and replaced."

I'd said it. The last sentence rang in my ears as if I had shouted it at the top of my voice. Something had just occurred that Wehrmacht regulations made no provision for: a colonel had demanded that his ultimate military superior be removed from his post! Von Greim could have had us arrested and court-martialed for mutiny. To my surprise, though, his face betrayed something more like amazement—possibly even a trace of amusement. Was he not going to take us seriously?

When he spoke it was in soothing tones. "But, gentlemen, the Reichsmarschall's reaction is understandable enough, is it not? Think of what he has to take from the Führer all the time. And every day the *Gauleiters* pester him with their 'Where are the fighters? Where's our air defense?'"

Franzl's lips were tightening in the way I knew so well and he thrust his great chin forward, eyes narrowed aggressively. But before he got his mouth open my own protest burst out of me:

"That's exactly what the Reichsmarschall says himself, sir! That's exactly the way he moans on at us—and he's the one to blame for the short-sighted planning of his so-called air defense. As a pilot I've seen both victories and defeats in this war, and what infuriates me is the phraseology we get dished out with instead of good, superior aircraft. He had well-trained, well-rested pilots confident of victory and prepared to risk their lives for it—he hasn't even got that anymore—and what did he call them? 'I know those old studs and cockatoos with and without Oak Leaves who make my life a misery—and I hate them!' "

Von Greim shot me an irritated glance and said nothing. Then Franzl started telling him about the group of commanders who had delegated us to put our case to him and ask his advice. He spoke of Galland's dismissal and of how this shelving of a man who was universally admired and respected had been as it were the straw that broke the camel's back. We had finally decided to stand up and be counted, he said, speaking rapidly and excitedly now, the words tumbling out of him:

"If the Reichsmarschall's complaint against the old studs and cockatoos is that they let their units run to seed and escape into the air merely in order to get away from having to grapple with problems of discipline and morale on the ground, why is his first question after every sortie: "Where was the commander flying—was he in the air?' When the four-engined bombers were coming in over the German Bay in April last year and he once asked whether the commander was flying he got the answer: 'No, he's in bed with a temperature.' 'Oh, yes,' he said, 'I've heard that one before. There's another of them has lost his nerve.' As you know, sir, Oberst O. was so furious at the insult that he climbed into his aircraft with a raging fever and flew off after his group. He's never been heard of since."

Von Greim shook his head indignantly. His chief of staff came in at that point and they whispered together for a few minutes. I caught occasional words—"breakthrough . . . pull back the front . . . snowstorm . . ." Then he went out again and von Greim, turning back to us, raised his eyebrows to indicate that we should go on.

"We've come to the conclusion that we must do something—take some action," I said. "We should like to ask you, sir, whether you would be prepared to take over the Luftwaffe in the Reichsmarschall's place. We want to put the matter to the Führer, even if it only gives us a chance to clear our consciences. . . ."

I broke off because von Greim had got to his feet and was pacing

up and down in front of the fireplace. He looked at the big grand-
father clock and said: "It is now only five hours to the morning sit.
report. If I tell you that it is too late, that what you propose has come
too late, I wish also to say that everything you have told me has
moved me most deeply. But as you saw this evening on the map, the
eastern front is now ablaze from the Baltic to Hungary. This is not
the beginning of the end—it *is* the end."

He sat down again and supported his head with both hands. His
eyes were rimmed with red and his face had a look of infinite tired-
ness.

"And now I want to tell you why I must reply to your request in
the negative. You know as well as I do that the Reichsmarschall's star
has been setting for some time now. The Führer has on numerous
occasions—particularly at sit. discussions—criticized him heavily. He
did so in a bitter and offensive manner—but also with a certain resignation, probably realizing that he could hardly drop his 'faithful paladin' at this stage of the proceedings. The army has been demanding
the Reichsmarschall's removal more and more urgently. It was not
until last autumn, however, that the Führer finally made up his mind
to put Göring on the shelf. He must have reached his decision in
September, because around the middle of the month I was summoned
to see the CGS. I was informed that the Führer wanted to make me
his Luftwaffe adviser, by which he effectively meant head of the Luftwaffe. Hitler thought Göring should remain nominal head for form's
sake, but as his deputy I would virtually have taken over everything.
The Reichsmarschall knew of the Führer's intentions, the CGS told
me, and had received the news without surprise, almost apathetically,
as if he had seen it coming.

"I flew straight off to see the Führer. The Reichsmarschall was not
in fact aware that he was being bypassed—and it must have made
him furious when he later found out. The Führer complained angrily
of what he called the total failure of the Luftwaffe, of the Reichsmarschall's incompetence, of the mendacity of his generals—well, I'd better spare you the details. I was to put forward proposals as to how the
Reichsmarschall could be left in office but at the same time stripped of
all authority. He wanted me to draw up a list of the powers I would
require.

"While I was writing my own service regulations, as it were, I received an order to report to the Reichsmarschall at Karinhall immedi-

ately. I arrived to find him so angry as to appear to have taken leave of his senses. In the cloud-cuckoo-land of his hunting-lodge he was once more the mighty creator of the Luftwaffe, pouring upon me the whole weight of his scorn. He had known for a long time that they were trying to shelve him, he told me, but that one of his own generals should be prepared to lend his support to this fiendish plan shocked him to the core. The whole intrigue would come to nothing—he would see to that! He had told the Führer so in no uncertain terms and convinced him that he, Göring, the founder and rightful head of the Luftwaffe, should retain his position and his powers unimpaired. And the Führer had agreed! I was to forget about the whole unseemly business and return to my air fleet immediately—period!"

He fell silent, and Franzl and I exchanged looks. We saw now how impossible it was for him to meet our request. We felt confused and suddenly very depressed, struck by the full hopelessness of our mission.

Von Greim stared into the dying fire, rubbing his massive forehead with both hands. Then, as if he had just that moment found words for what was tormenting him, he got up heavily and began pacing to and fro in the semidarkness behind our chairs. There was an edge to his voice now.

"Gentlemen, I ask you to appreciate what a wretched position all this has put me in. I who have served the Reichsmarschall faithfully for many years. Who have believed in the Führer—and, damn it, still believe in him. At least I try to—you can take it from me—difficult as they make it for one in a situation like this. . . . Well, you saw for yourselves this evening. And it's been going on like that since Stalingrad—always on the retreat, always fresh defeats, fresh disappointments, miscalculations, orders no one can carry out . . . You've no idea of the things I have to force myself to sign. One simply has to believe—I mean one needs this faith like a rock in order to survive it all. What you go through in your units I have here a hundred times over! And then this . . . this unreasonable demand on the Führer's part, and the Reichsmarschall's withering scorn, and the CGS picking his way gingerly between them. And the lookout for my air fleet becoming daily more hopeless. No, gentlemen—you're asking too much of me. I can't become a traitor. I just can't. And least of all against Hermann Göring. Do you understand that? I can't do it."

His voice failed him and he sank into his armchair, pressing his

fists to his eyes and forehead and breathing heavily. I did not dare to
look at Franzl Lützow, but from his direction I heard a vague sound
very much like a sob. I felt uncomfortably tight-throated myself, hearing a soldier I had so much respect for talk like that. God, what a
mess we were all in!

We sat in silence, gazing at the dying embers. Only when the storm
outside whistled in the chimney did the fire spring to life once more
in a brief dance of blue flame. Each of us was privately groping in the
darkness of his own thoughts and forebodings. I sensed terrible events
bearing ineluctably down on us. Outside the blizzard howled. From
the corridor came the muffled sounds of a command staff in a state
of hectic activity. On the map in the next room the disasters at the
front would be assuming the abstract form of little blue and red sym-
bols. I felt cold all of a sudden.

When von Greim looked up at us there was something like sympathy in his eyes. He gave me the impression that the whole thing had
nothing to do with him anymore; it was we who counted. He laid a
hand on my arm and began to speak again very seriously and quietly,
leaning forward lest we miss anything.

"It would be unfair of me not to tell you that I received prior notice
of your arrival. You have placed your trust in me in a way I hardly
deserve. If I tell you that I had a telephone call from the Chief of the
Luftwaffe General Staff it is because I trust you not to tell another
soul."

Franzl and I exchanged an appalled look. With a shock that was
almost like a physical blow I realized the danger we were in. But who
could have given us away? We had chosen our group with care.

"Koller told me on the phone about the crisis of confidence in the
Jagdwaffe. He thoroughly disapproves of what you're doing, of
course, but above all of the way you're going about it. He wants you
to go and see him as soon as you get back because, as he says, a
catastrophe must be avoided. He's thinking of what happened on 20
July.

"Gentlemen, what you have told me is terrible, hopeless, and depressing. But I can think of no other advice to give you than that you
go and see the CGS and pour out your hearts to him. You will appreciate now why you cannot count on me to take charge of the Luftwaffe. And I say again what I said after the sit. report: it's too late.

Now I'm going to have a word with Koller. You'd better get a couple of hours' sleep."

He rose, gave us his hand, and walked wearily to the door.

We had leapt to our feet and were left standing alone in the middle of the dimly lit room. Though our eyes met, neither of us spoke. Franzl Lützow suddenly looked old and ill. I was aware of a measureless exhaustion. Our mission had failed.

From the diary of General Koller

13 January 1945, 14.45 hours

Have just heard that the Jagdwaffe is in the throes of a major crisis of confidence regarding its supreme commander.

Some very bad feeling indeed. The most impossible ideas being thrown around. Occurrences similar to those of 20 July must be avoided.

Commanders want to get to the Führer without the Reichsmarschall's knowledge. It is being suggested that the supreme commander should resign. . . .

Oberst Lützow and Oberst Steinhoff have flown to see Generaloberst von Greim.

Pointed out to go-between that the whole thing was militarily impossible. Talk of forcing a supreme commander to resign his post amounts to mutiny . . .

Told go-between that I would be getting in touch with von Greim to put him in the picture before Lützow and Steinhoff arrived. Also told him I must make a proper report about the crisis of confidence to my supreme commander . . .

14 January 1945, 1.45 hours

GREIM (on the phone): "That the men came to me to get it off their chests and ask me to mediate for them I don't think anyone can hold against them. They are honorably concerned to find a way out of their difficulties. And it is intolerable, what's happening. The men will be in touch with you as soon as they get back to Berlin. I recommend taking no action against them for the moment . . .

─────────────

I'm not saying I bear no blame myself. The chief thing I'm to blame for is not having given the Jagdwaffe heavy-caliber defensive weapons early enough and having failed to grasp the importance of the Flying Fortresses in time. . . .

. . . I didn't say all fighter pilots were cowards. But I do reckon they've lost their nerve—you can depend on that.

Hermann Göring
From the minutes of a discussion
with the Reichsmarschall,
Obersalzberg, 7 October 1943

─────────────

6
Berlin
19 January 1945

On 17 January Lützow and I were finally summoned to see General Koller, the Chief of the Luftwaffe General Staff. He had just that day returned from operational HQ in the west, so it was not that he had found some excuse to keep us waiting three days. But would he not have informed Göring as soon as our plans had been betrayed to him?

Actually, all we wanted from him was a mere formality. He was aware of the various stages of our plan and knew that the only thing left to us was a confrontation with Göring, our attempt to reach Hitler by a shortcut via the SS having proved a dismal failure, and von Greim having now shown us that he was in no position to help either. But we were still extremely nervous, because the way Koller reacted to our request would be an indication of whether they were going to take us seriously and organize a meeting with Göring—or whether they were going to put an end to the whole business right away by having us arrested.

As soon as we were face to face with the CGS we knew they were prepared to negotiate (or hush things up?). The tall, powerful Bavarian with the coarse-featured face adopted a fatherly tone, asking at full volume: "Now, gentlemen, what seems to be the trouble?" His words carried a confidential undertone, although he was careful to preserve a certain distance as if to say: I am the great CGS and you are mere frontline officers.

I then witnessed the humiliating spectacle of Franzl Lützow being obliged to trot out the whole list of our preoccupations and demands although both he and I knew for a fact that Koller had been told all about them long before and had precise knowledge of our objectives. The state of the Jagdwaffe, what in our opinion ought to be done about stopping the bomb terror, the tragedy of the Me 262 jet fighter, the insulting behavior of the Reichsmarschall and the incompetence of his entourage—Franzl had to reel it all off yet again. I threw in a remark here and there and did a bit of underlining as and when I thought necessary.

When we had finished Koller said, "But this is an impossible way of going about things! This is conspiracy, if not actual mutiny!"

But there was no threat in his voice; he was saying it because he had to, for form's sake.

We had been going on at him without a pause, deeply serious and occasionally breaking out in anger. Now, having ended, we both felt that we had a strong case and that at least they must listen to us.

"Of course you must tell the Reichsmarschall what's bothering you," Koller went on. "But if I arrange a meeting straight away, do please bear in mind the very difficult position he's in at the moment. . . ."

But he got no further with these banalities because we pounced on him—aggressive now—with arguments: "Yes, sir, we know—'If they get through to the capital, my name's Meier!' Amateurish bungling, no real concern for the Luftwaffe, calling his fighter pilots names. . . ."

This was too much for Koller. He cut us off sharply:

"I shall be in touch with the Reichsmarschall immediately to ask him to give you an appointment, gentlemen."

From the diary of General Koller

"Morale in the Jagdwaffe"

Luftwaffe High Command,   HQ 17.1.45
The Chief of the General Staff.   23.50 hours
No. 1202/45 g.Kdos.
To the Reichsmarschall of the Pan-German Reich, Supreme
Commander of the Luftwaffe.
     I beg to report as follows:
     For some time a mood of increasing depression has been observable

in the Jagdwaffe, particularly among certain commanding officers. . . .
This now appears to have reached a point where it has become critical.

The causes of this increasing bad feeling are, as I see them:

A deep feeling of bitterness at the continued charge of cowardice. Lack
of confidence in the direction of operations. . . . Lack of confidence in the
Luftwaffe high command with regard to armament, concentration of
forces, personnel policy, and leadership of the Luftwaffe generally. . . .

Objection is taken to the dismissal of Galland, behind whom the
Jagdwaffe stands virtually to a man.

Apparently remarks have been made that are directed against the
Supreme Commander personally. There appear to have been plans to
bypass the Supreme Commander and, in some cases using services
outside the Luftwaffe, gain access to the Führer in order to inform him
directly of the problems that exist and offer suggestions for dealing with
them.

Arising out of this general depression and no doubt acting in all
sincerity and prompted by the best intentions, Oberst Lützow and Oberst
Steinhoff, with the knowledge of other officers, asked Generaloberst von
Greim as senior Jagdwaffe officer for an interview and went to see von
Greim on 13 January. I was informed of this development on the
afternoon of 13 January at 15.00 hours . . .

I was able to inform Generaloberst von Greim accordingly by
telephone before the meeting took place and agree that he should contact
me again afterward.

He did so on 14 January at 01.45 hours . . .

On my return today, 17 January, at 14.00 hours from advanced
operations HQ in the west, the men requested an interview as expected.
Lützow, Steinhoff, and Rödel arrived at 17.30 hours. Our discussion
confirmed what I said at the beginning of my report about morale among
Jagdwaffe personnel.

In order to contain developments for the time being I informed the
above-named officers that I would try to arrange for you, *Herr
Reichsmarschall*, to receive a number of leading Jagdwaffe officers for a
frank discussion and further that I would ask you, Sir, if on individual
points this should be necessary, to arrange an appointment with the
Führer.

It is my impression that a serious crisis of confidence is developing
that, if nothing is done to halt it, may lead to very serious tension and
eventually to catastrophe. At the present stage of the war this must under
all circumstances be prevented.

I therefore suggest receiving the above-mentioned officers for a frank
discussion in order to clear the air . . .

(Signed) KOLLER

On 19 January—we had spent the two days in a state of considerable nervous excitement—the order came through that we should stand by to meet the Reichsmarschall for a discussion at the *Haus der Flieger*, the Luftwaffe club in Berlin.

The nearer this "moment of truth" approached, the more soberly I found myself viewing the situation. The confrontation with Göring was occurring at a time when the Luftwaffe had practically ceased to exist as a force that the Allied bombers needed to reckon with at all seriously as they went about their work of wearing down the Reich's resistance. And since on top of this the fighter reserve built up with such energy and determination by Galland had been senselessly dissipated in the useless and ineffective offensive operation known as "Bedplate" that Göring had ordered on 1 January, the prospects for any sort of concentric, effective defense in the air looked pretty gloomy. We were faced with the fact that at the beginning of 1945 the whole of Germany was exposed virtually without protection to the raids of the Allied bombers. For them it was not a question of what they were in a position to destroy but of deciding what to destroy first. And since they encountered no resistance in the air and were able to reach every corner of the now shrunken Reich, they accomplished veritable superlatives of destruction.

The night before the capital had been attacked by Mosquitoes, as it was virtually every night. The performance never varied. These extraordinarily fast, high-flying bombers (built of wood, they had been designed originally as high-speed reconnaissance aircraft), heading in from the British Isles, triggered off our air-raid warning system as soon as they reached the Elbe. There were usually no more than four or five of them, but they drove the entire city down into the air-raid shelters.

By staggering their arrival times and using different approach routes they not only kept our antiaircraft gunners on their toes but robbed Berliners of their sleep nearly every night. They dropped air mines—clumsy great things as big as oil drums—and they dropped them indiscriminately because they were incapable of hitting even a large target with any degree of accuracy.

Night after night the Mosquitoes bit Berlin, and our powerlessness against them was depressing.

From the minutes of a discussion with the Reichsmarschall,
Obersalzberg, 7 October 1943

REICHSMARSCHALL: You've got to get those Mosquitoes! The X-beam or
Y-beam or whatever it's called* may be all right for individual intrusions.
But if it's going to go on like this, with Mosquitoes flitting about the
place with absolute impunity, then as far as I'm concerned it means our
people can pack up and get out, beams and all, because either this beam
works, in which case it must inevitably lead the fighter straight to the
Mosquito . . . But what makes me furious is when a Mosquito flies in on
the dot for a night raid—and gets away with it! Look—the man [i.e., the
Mosquito pilot] has only one course. It's like fox-hunting: I know I've
stopped up three holes, so the fox has to come out of the fourth. I'd have
to be a bloody awful hunter not to get the fox then. But the Mosquitoes
get away with it. It's despicable, it really is.

It was a wet, cold winter's day as I drove into Berlin. Snow and rain
appeared to be working shifts, and the roads were covered with a
deep layer of slush.

We gathered outside the building. At our suggestion all the conspirators had been summoned to Berlin who a month before had decided
to take action: Lützow, Trautloft, Neumann, Rödel, and Steinhoff.
They had tried to get two or three other commanders from Reich
Defense, the eastern front, or the English Channel—to form a count-
erpole, as it were, or to hear the voice of the front—but the meeting
had been fixed at such short notice that this had proved impossible.

We were shown into a small conference room containing a large
round table, and we were left to wait for Göring. The room was overheated and the humidity condensed on the big windows and ran
down in long streaks. The wet snow, flung against the panes, melted
on contact. I wondered if his idea was to wear us down with waiting.

Lützow stood stiffly behind his chair, looking straight ahead. He
was to be our spokesman. The others exchanged trivial remarks and
tried to pretend the whole affair was of no importance.

How would Göring take it? I had seen him as the condescending
father of his air force, a man who inhabited Olympian heights and

---

*A navigational and assault aid for night fighters, using a concentrated radio beam
aimed at the located enemy (*J.S.*).

referred to young officers as *Pimpfe.** I had seen him with coat flapping open and marshal's baton in hand, peering through a periscope across the Channel toward Dover. And I had heard him the previous October when, before an audience, he cynically, insultingly, and vulgarly hauled his fighter pilots over the coals and denounced them as cowards.

Why did I feel so powerful an aversion to the man? I had begun erecting my personal wall of inner resistance to him shortly after the beginning of the war when I became aware that our idol played with us young officers like a cat with its kittens, seeing us as his chattels, his own personal property—us and his entire Luftwaffe. To keep myself from succumbing to the power of his personality I had trained myself into an increasingly critical attitude. I began to see his faults with crystal clarity, and I experienced something approaching shame at the fact that I had once allowed myself to be swept off my feet by him.

It was in the summer of 1936. My year had just been promoted lieutenant and we had been summoned to Berlin to be addressed by the Supreme Commander of the Luftwaffe. We assembled in the *Preussenhaus*, the old Prussian parliament building, where we filled the semicircular rows of oak benches—several hundred young men in the blue uniforms of the new Luftwaffe. We were the Luftwaffe's first lieutenant year since the inauguration of the Third Reich—lads who had become soldiers immediately on leaving school and others who, like myself, had interrupted their university studies because they could not resist the temptation of being allowed to fly, and because even the academic professions offered very limited prospects at that time. Maybe five hundred lieutenants waited there for their chief, waited for the war hero, the last commander of the celebrated Richthofen Squadron, holder of the *"Pour le Mérite"* order, the living legend we used to call the "Iron Man." Every child in the country knew the man who had joined Hitler early on and whose incontestable popularity Hitler had made adroit use of ("my faithful paladin"). Although Göring's love of show, his theatrical bent, and his boastfulness were already evident and the occasion of numerous jokes, he still en-

---

*"Squirts"; the word was applied in the NS period to members of the Hitler Youth (*Tr.*).

joyed the favor of the masses; they did not begrudge the famous flier
and tireless campaigner for Hitler his little extravagances.

As he mounted the podium and began to speak to "his lieutenants," his ringing, challenging voice effortlessly filled the large semicircular hall. From the start he as it were rolled up his sleeves and
made quite clear to us that he was addressing men who belonged to
him. "You," he told us, "are now officers in my Luftwaffe. I want
you to know why this powerful, independent air force was created by
me in the first place."

He went back a long way, and before we realized what was happening we were involved in dogfights in the sky above Flanders. He
talked of knightly jousts with the British and French, of the superiority and moral vigor of the Germans, and of that virtuoso of the dogfight, Baron von Richthofen. We positively hung on his lips as he
explained, as if it had been the most natural thing in the world, that
our job would be to fight, shoot, drop bombs—and kill. Aerial combat—"when you flash past the enemy so close that you can see the
whites of his eyes"—was transformed in his vivid account until, from
being a grim fight to the death, it came to resemble some medieval
courtly entertainment. His hands gesticulated, and in his face, which
had already started to swell up and lose its shape, I suddenly caught
again that look of bold determination that had characterized it in his
younger years. Like a figure of Wagnerian opera he conjured up before our eyes an almost tangible image of his new Romantic ideal—
the knight of the technological age.

Then he spoke of the years in which he had thrown in his lot with
Hitler, of the betrayal of the German people at the front by left-wing
elements at home, and of the failure of the Weimar Republic. He told
us how the Great Powers had sought with the help of the *Diktat* of
Versailles to humiliate and permanently weaken Germany, and how
the perfidious way in which our great nation had been stripped of its
colonies was typically, despicably Anglo-Saxon. In moving terms he
accused the victorious powers of wanting to throw the German people—"*Ein Volk ohne Raum,*" a people lacking living-space—in
chains and break its spirit. But the superior Germanic race was not
going to let itself be bound by *Untermenschen*, by its racial inferiors.
And he began to talk of the future, of the resurrection of the Pan-
German Reich and the restoration of its historic frontiers—and of a
"settling of accounts" with those who had dictated to us at Versailles.

We were familiar with anti-Versailles polemics and the "stab-in-the-back" legend, but we listened with bated breath.

At army college we had been taught to obey—and it had not been exactly gentle persuasion, either. The attempt to "break our will and instill the inviolability of orders in our blood" had been crowned with success.

So Göring had his hearers well under his thumb when in a voice sharp with command—like a bugle sounding the attack—he shouted: "One of these days you'll be my vengeance corps!"

Hearing the door open behind me, I turned to find myself looking Göring in the face. It was a weary face, bloated and with folds like an old woman's falling from the mouth to the double chin, which in turn folded over the pale blue uniform collar encircling the massive neck. His flaccid skin showed traces of pink powder.

We leapt to attention and saluted as the colossus made his way to the head of the table, followed by his escort: the CGS and his adjutant, several general-staff officers, and two shorthand writers. Göring was wearing the ordinary Luftwaffe uniform; we were used to seeing him more imaginatively dressed. Koller and his adjutant flanked him as he took his seat. Behind him, their knees drawn up because there was so little room, sat the shorthand writers, armed with thick writing-pads and batteries of sharpened pencils projecting from their breast pockets like organ pipes. They would be taking down every word we said. In order that we could be called to account afterward ("My dear fellow, you said on that occasion—and I quote . . .") and that *he* would be covered. Clearly his escort would be hung rather than open their mouths, let alone join in our impassioned indictment. ("But aren't you dramatizing rather? I mean, you're not the only ones fighting this war . . .") I recalled his words back in October over a year before, during the discussion up at Obersalzberg, when it had been a question yet again of laying the blame for the catastrophic bomb terror on the "cowardly" fighter pilots.

From the minutes of a discussion with the Reichsmarschall, Obersalzberg, 7 October 1943

GÖRING: A great many of our fighter pilots, the young ones, have been spoiled by the jaded old studs with or without Oak Leaves . . .
VOICE: They should be court-martialed . . . shot . . .

GÖRING: Aging, overweight cockatoos. . . . I remember them from the World War. I loathe them—I wish I was rid of them. I can think of a few squadron leaders and wing commanders I should have had up before a court-martial long ago. . . .

In fact he was the only fat one among us. And our excesses were nothing compared with his own megalomanic extravagance.

Lützow sat bolt upright, our manifesto on the table in front of him. His thin-lipped mouth, drawn down slightly at the corners, made the big square jaw look even harder and his face even more congenial. Trautloft too sat rigid in his chair, towering above the rest of us even when seated. And there was A., the only bomber commodore, who had been admitted to our circle because his group had been re-equipped as fighters and because he was our principal witness as far as rebutting the charge of cowardice was concerned. Though placid and easy-going in his movements and manner, he was far from fat and he was certainly no cockatoo. Moreover, he would speak up for us today—of that I was certain.

We and the other conspirators had spent hours wrestling over that manifesto the day before. The hotheads had wanted it to be accusatory in tone and dogmatic in its demands. Trautloft had counseled moderation. In fact the manifesto was of no consequence whatever, now that our plans had been betrayed. But only Lützow and I knew that, so for form's sake we had joined in the endless discussion of document that was ultimately not worth the paper it was written on.

Lützow had now pulled it from his breast pocket and spread it out on the table before him. Copies of the same memorandum—"Points for Discussion"—lay in front of Göring and Koller.

Göring shot a mildly irritated glance round the table and then turned to look questioningly at the CGS. Apart from a strained "Good morning, gentlemen" (no "Heil Hitler!") he had taken no notice of us—not even a friendly nod for his group commanders. But nor was there any of the arrogance with which he had insultingly snubbed me at a discussion about night-fighter operations four years before ("You have no say here; you're too young"). There was even a trace of uncertainty, of uneasy curiosity.

"Herr Reichsmarschall," Koller began, "I wrote to you that a number of group commanders from the Jagdwaffe had asked me if they might have a frank discussion with you. The gentlemen would like you to accept Oberst Lützow as their spokesman."

Göring nodded and turned to Lützow who, rising to his feet and returning Göring's look with an air almost of challenge, pitched straight in:

"*Herr Reichsmarschall*, we are grateful to you for agreeing to listen to our problems. I must ask you, however, to hear me out to the end. If you interrupt me, sir, I believe there will be little point to this discussion."

Franzl had come boldly out with the sentence that had been giving him such headaches. ("He won't hear me out—he'll cut me off in the middle of what I have to say. He's never listened to anyone for any length of time, barring the Führer. I've got to make it clear to him right from the start that we're deadly serious about this.")

The most striking thing about the pause that followed was that Göring stared at Lützow as if turned to stone and said nothing at all. The CGS too had never heard anything like it from a junior officer and tried by sitting absolutely still to convey an impression of complete neutrality, while the adjutant stared fixedly at the tabletop. (He must have known we were asking that the Reichsmarschall change his "personal entourage.")

"*Herr Reichsmarschall*," Lützow went on, "your fighter pilots, particularly the day fighters, are extremely concerned about the immediate future of their service and their chances of playing an effective part in the defense of the Reich. We are aware that you, sir, come in for heavy criticism on account of the alleged failure of the Jagdwaffe. You for your part have had no hesitation in passing that criticism on to us by accusing us of 'loss of nerve' and even at times of cowardice."

This was strong medicine; it was almost as if Lützow had been provoking the Reichsmarschall to interrupt. But precisely in order to stop him doing so he went on in his firmest voice:

"Your Jagdwaffe is still in a position to relieve the country by putting at least a temporary stop to the bomb terror. We believe, however, that this means concentrating all efforts on fighter operations as systematically as possible. Things like the dismissal of General Galland, the former General of Fighter Pilots, seem to us to be barking up the wrong tree. On the contrary, the leadership of this strengthened Jagdwaffe must be in the hands of experienced fighter pilots who have proved their worth in this war. Success will depend on our assembling all available forces and using them in a concentrated fashion. This means that the reserve bomber units detailed for fighter operations must be placed under experienced Jagdwaffe officers, and we demand that all Me 262 jet aircraft be released immediately for fighter operations. With properly planned, concentrated assault work, the Jagdwaffe could deliver blows of a kind that would force the enemy to think twice about his plan to destroy our cities and possibly even call a halt to the bomb terror.

"We are familiar with your critical remarks about the morale and achievements of this service. But we ask you, sir, to consider the bloodletting that the Jagdwaffe has suffered in four years of war. . . ."

The strain on Göring's tolerance and self-control must have been enormous. Lützow really seemed to be out to get his goat, and in fact Göring did at this point drop his beringed right hand with an audible slap on the memorandum before him, the corners of his mouth beginning to twitch. But Lützow, his voice ringing with confidence, left him no chance to interrupt.

"The Jagdwaffe, sir, represented here by a number of group commanders, feels deeply humiliated. It believes the time has come for a series of false decisions to be systematically put right. It is prepared neither to accept the charge of cowardice nor to contemplate any longer the spectacle of fully manned bomber units—the IXth Corps, for example—being held inactive in reserve and fitted out with jet aircraft while what is left of the Jagdwaffe bleeds to death. There is still time, sir, to prevent every city in Germany from being reduced to rubble and ashes."

A dangerously red-faced Göring, visibly struggling for breath, slammed his palm down hard on the tabletop several times. Lützow did not have a hope of continuing his phillipic now. Not that he even seemed to want to at this point, instead looking Göring steadily in the eye until the latter began to speak.

"Now wait a minute, gentlemen—this is pretty strong stuff you're dishing out here."

His tone was still astonishingly restrained. He had of course prepared himself for this appearance. (Fatherly understanding to start with, then a bit of a moan—"Look, you're letting me down"—and finally the thunderclap: "Now will you kindly return to your units and start doing your duty, namely shooting down enemy aircraft." No admissions, no readiness to see our point of view.)

"Do you think I'm blind?" he went on. "Do you think I don't

realize how much I'm asking of you?" Then, however, he dropped his first brick. "But you've also been pampered and made much of for long enough, fêted as national heroes—I'm thinking of the battle for England and those dubious kill figures. . . ."

Lützow, who had remained on his feet, suddenly drew his brow down aggressively and opened his mouth to protest. Realizing his mistake, Göring hurried on:

"But [why "but"?—none of us had said anything] you [fatherly, but already more in the manner of a feudal lord to his villeins] have to admit that some of your units are in a deplorable state. You want the jets, you want the bomber groups taken into the Jagdwaffe. . . . Well, I recently visited a bomber unit and it was a heartening sight, I can tell you—discipline, organization, a thoroughly soldierly-looking outfit. They're also more experienced, can fly in bad weather. . . ."

Lützow could not take any more. He was not prepared to be told the same old story for the *n*th time over. Disrespectfully loud and in a tone almost of contempt he broke in:

"*Herr Reichsmarschall* [and—when a nettled Göring still tried to continue—again louder:] *Herr Reichsmarschall*, so you have told us time and time again. You forget that we fighter pilots have been flying missions daily for over five years now. You forget that you can hardly expect fighter units to look as if they're on parade the whole time when they are being pushed around from pillar to post like gypsies and when you can practically count the survivors of five years' war on the fingers of one hand. Many groups are already commanded by former NCOs, and our young pilots survive a maximum of two or three Reich Defense missions before they're killed. We're bled dry, sir. The transfer of the bomber groups with their still-sound manpower reserves is vital for us and for our whole air defense—that is, if it isn't too late already. . . ."

At this there was no holding Göring. His authoritarian nature had already had to swallow too much insubordination. His stentorian voice rang out in fury:

"As if the head of the Luftwaffe [meaning himself] was not aware of that! But rather than risk having my bomber pilots become as dead-beat as my fighter pilots I'll go on keeping them in reserve. I don't deny that individual fighter pilots do a grand job, but that doesn't make them military leaders, and on the ground their units just run to seed."

From the minutes of a discussion held at Obersalzberg on 28 May 1944. Subject: "The State of Reich Defense"

REICHSMARSCHALL: Here I knock myself out doing fantastic things, supplying the "Reich" air fleet with hundreds upon hundreds of machines, and I get a miserable "ready for action" report of a few paltry aircraft. It's just too bad, it really is. Our wing and group commanders are simply not good enough. Their hearts just aren't in it. My group commanders don't seem to like flying so much, Galland—they'd rather play with themselves on the ground!

"There's no system to the way you fight," Göring ranted on. "You haven't trained your fighter pilots to go right up to the bombers and give them on quarter. When I think back to our days and the war in Flanders . . ."

Almost shouting this time, Lützow broke in: "And you, sir, have simply ignored the existence of four-engined bombers completely. You've given us no new aircraft, no new weapons . . ."

Shaken, Göring looked for a moment as if he might acknowledge Lützow's rebuke, but then his anger got the better of him: "Don't you take that tone with me, Lützow! Anyone would think I'd never smelt powder. I don't need your advice—what I need are fighter pilots who are falling all over themselves for a crack at the enemy. Your tactics are pathetic. You're a match for the bombers any time, but what it takes is for as many fighters as possible to be thrown against the bomber formation and fire at it with everything they've got. And it has to be done at point-blank range." Whereupon he launched into a theatrical lecture about his conception of the tactics of aerial combat, not without invoking the glorious example of those chivalrous engagements in the Flanders sky. ("Of course many things have changed since then—but despite all the equipment and technical refinements that you have in your aircraft, what counts is the man, the fighting individual.")

He told us he wanted the bomber streams kept under continuous attack from the moment they entered the Reich's air space to the moment they left it again. The Jagdwaffe, he said, had still not satisfactorily carried out his order to strike at the enemy as often as possible during an intrusion.

From the minutes of a discussion held at the Air Ministry, Berlin, in July 1944. Subject: "Reich Defense"

REICHSMARSCHALL: . . . What is decisive is that as many aircraft as possible should be thrown against the enemy formation at one go—that they really get in close and fire away with everything they've got. And then the moment the ammunition runs out, down they dive to the nearest airfield—I'll let them do that!—for immediate reloading. Once they've reloaded, and once a squadron has been gotten together again, the attack must be resumed straight away. . . . I can see that a more extended type of engagement, i.e., one in which the enemy is hit over and over again, is going to be useful because the enemy will tire a lot and because it will force him to use up more ammunition. . . .

What he was asking of us had never—not even in the days when we had the men and machines to pursue such tactics—been more than a desperate attempt to clobber the enemy wherever he appeared over the Reich. The attempt, however, had soon turned out to be impractible as well as involving exceptionally heavy losses. Above all it was the psychological demands placed on the pilots that set limits to the tactics of permanent assault. Granted, it had proved possible in one or two cases, following the "first strike," hurriedly to assemble a few formations at the airfields where the pilots had come down. But the success of the second and third "strikes" had been small. Those of us who had prepared and flown missions against phalanxes of *Viermots* with their bristling arsenal of weapons knew just how questionable was the reckless watchword: "Keep them under constant attack as long as you can still fight and stay in the air, right down to the last man and the last shell in your magazines."

At a wave from Göring, Lützow had sat down. The Reichsmarschall was in a hurry now and wanted to get things over with. The "discussion" had taken the turn we had feared it would, with Göring lecturing to us in a way that was deliberately beside the point.

Now, however, Franzl spoke up again: "*Herr Reichsmarschall,* you have seen our discussion points. We should be glad to have your opinion. . . ."

This was what Göring had wanted to avoid. Probably he had had no intention of entering into a discussion in the first place. In fact he seemed to feel that enough talking had been done already; the mutineers had had a chance to "let off steam" and now it was up to him to sort things out again by issuing a few orders (and at the same time consider what was to be done about these refractory and rebellious officers). Picking up our memorandum between thumb and forefinger and tossing it into the middle of the table, Göring said, "What is this preposterous rubbish—funny little bits of paper with 'Points for Discussion' on . . . ? What's gotten into you anyway, that you dare to take such a liberty with me?"

Hesitantly we coauthors of the memorandum began to speak up, saying that we fully endorsed everything Lützow had said, that we were deeply disturbed, and that our fighter units really were in a pitiful state—through absolutely no fault of our own. My mention of the jet fighter really seemed to be the last straw as far as Göring was concerned.

"Now let me tell you something, gentlemen." (All trace of father-feeling had disappeared from his now official, ice-cold voice.) "Your insolence in this matter positively defies belief. You presume to dictate to me how I should be running my Luftwaffe. And you go on stubbornly repeating the same thing over and over again, although I've told you what is possible and what I am not prepared to do." (He had told us nothing of the kind; he had been beating about the bush, avoiding everything he did not like the look of.) "You are asking me to put everything in together, concentrate everything including my bombers. Well, that's exactly what I am not going to do! I'd be a fool not to keep this powerful, magnificent reserve for the moment when I decide to strike the decisive blow. You want the Me 262 and you're not going to get it because I'm giving it to the people who know what to do with it, namely my bomber pilots.

"And now a word about your request that I leave General Galland in his post as General of Fighter Pilots. I respect him enormously, he is a most worthy officer, but he occupied the post for years—too long, actually. He is in need of rest and relaxation . . ."

Lützow paled, and his fingers began to drum nervously on the tabletop. It made me feel ill myself, hearing the old litany yet again, but this time Lützow lost all control of himself. He leapt to his feet, shouting, "*Herr Reichsmarschall . . .*"

"I'm talking now, Lützow, I'm talking now! And let me tell you

right away what I think of this whole business! What you're present-
ing me with here, gentlemen, is treason—mutiny! It's absolutely monstrous that you should conspire behind my back to pursue devious
paths that represent a grave infringement of your duty as soldiers and
your obligation of loyalty to me. I shall take appropriate action!"

(So he knew everything, he knew every step of our undertaking,
and he would have his revenge.)

"Not only do you deceive me but you openly foster defeatism," he
ranted on. "You demand that I change my staff and you dare to criti-
cize me personally."

He was positively aglow with anger, coming out with all the things
he had in fact meant to keep from us when he was still acting on the
assumption that we could be frightened into eating humble pie.

"Instead of sitting on your arses hatching plots you should be with
your units, leading them against the enemy! But all you do is grouse
around, spoil my youngsters for me, and undermine the morale of my
troops . . ."

Lützow was standing behind his chair, staring at Göring with a
look almost of hatred. His face revealed his disappointment at the
fact that things had turned out worse than we had feared.

"What are you after, Lützow—do you want to get rid of me? What
you've schemed up here is a full-scale mutiny. I'd like to know what
your father would say if he heard what you've been doing . . ."

"I talked everything over with my father yesterday evening," retorted Lützow. "My action—our action—has his unqualified approval."

"That's enough!" Göring roared. "I don't wish to hear any more!
You're all mad and I propose to treat you accordingly. You! Lützow!
For an officer you have an incredible conception of your duty as a
soldier . . ." Placing his fat hands on the table, he pushed back his
chair and stood up. His face was crimson. "Lützow, you . . . you . . .
I'll have you shot!" And with a final lordly sweep of his gold-beringed
hand that condemned us all outright he rampaged out of the room,
followed by his dazed clique. I caught a glance from the CGS that
contained something approaching sympathy.

The five of us, left alone, stood around the table as if transfixed.
No one spoke. We hardly dared to look at one another. The wet snow
was still slapping at the windowpanes. The overheated room struck
me as intolerably small. I felt as if I were in prison already. Any mo-

ment now the guard detachment would come in and arrest us. It was obvious what would follow: detention without badges or bootlaces, court-martial . . .

But nothing happened.

Gradually the tension slipped away. We looked at one another in silence, an uncertain shrug here, a puzzled shake of the head there. When still nothing happened, I asked, "What now?"

No one answered. Then Franzl Lützow, from whom the excitement of the last hour appeared to have dropped like a discarded garment, said:

"Oh well, let's go and get something to eat."

Oberst "Edu" Neumann, who belonged to the inner circle of the rebel fighter pilots, was "*Jagdfliegerführer Oberitalien*," that is to say he commanded the Italian fighter units from a mountaintop headquarters not far from Verona. There were two Italian fighter groups at this stage of the war, both flying Me 109 aircraft. There had been no German fighter pilots left on Italian soil for some time. Neumann had managed to build up a relationship of enormous trust with those Italian fighter pilots who, in the far from easy situation in which they found themselves, with their country split into two camps since the king and Badoglio's secession from the Axis, nevertheless wanted to go on fighting with us till the end. He had been ordered to Berlin for the discussion with Göring and planned to take the furlough train back to Italy the same evening.

Letting himself into his Berlin flat that afternoon, Neumann heard the telephone ringing. He lifted the receiver and gave his name. A colonel at Personnel gave his and asked straight out, "When are you thinking of returning to Italy?"

"I'm taking the daily furlough train," Neumann replied. "It leaves at 22.30 hours."

"Please don't leave your flat," the colonel ordered. "I shall be ringing back."

Neumann was scared stiff. Convinced that Göring was now about to strike, he took immediate steps to warn the rest of us. He was still trying to reach Lützow and myself—I was on the way back to Gatow, where I was staying at the guest barracks—when an order arrived there for me to report to the Head of Luftwaffe Personnel at 10.00 hours the following morning. In fact I had just finished reading the order when the telephone rang and Neumann's voice said, "Macky, I've been told not to leave my flat. I've got a feeling they're serious this time. Where's Franzl? Do please warn him . . ."

"I'm to report to the Head of Personnel tomorrow morning," I told him. "They'll surely leave us alone till then . . ."

So Neumann sat in his flat for several tense hours until around eight in the evening the same colonel rang again and announced laconically, "You'll not be traveling to Italy today. Report to the Head of Personnel at 10.30 hours tomorrow."

When the furlough train drew out of Berlin's Anhalt station at half past ten that evening, Oberst Lützow, occupying the private compartment that the military police had reserved for him, settled down for the journey that was to take him into banishment in Italy. He was taking over from Neumann as "*Jagdfliegerführer Oberitalien*" and had strict orders not to try and contact any of the "mutineers."

Entering the Head of Personnel's outer office next morning, I passed Galland in the doorway. "Don't let them make you any indecent proposals, Macky. They wanted to give me a division in the east. I turned it down flat—and now I'm out of a job."

The Head of Luftwaffe Personnel, General M., did not seem particularly pleased to have been given the job of scattering us to the four winds. As I took the seat across the desk from him he launched into an irrelevant speech about "wear and tear after so many years at the front" and about the need to train the younger generation of officers. Not a word about the real reason for this multiple transfer operation. Instead he was almost paternal in this manner—full of good advice and actually seeming to care about me. Perhaps he even meant it all sincerely.

"What would you like to do next, then? Don't you think it would be a good deal if you went to the Luftwaffe Academy and became a really useful general-staff officer?"

I had my answer all ready: "I'd like to have back the group that was taken away from me in such undignified circumstances. I turned down my transfer to the Academy two years ago. Today, sir, at five minutes to midnight, the idea of taking it up again strikes me as absurd. I want to fly—all I want is to fly."

The general looked offended but said nothing. Then, getting to his feet, he announced, "The Reichsmarschall has given orders that you are not to command a flying unit. . . ." He paused. (Another "jaded old stud with Oak Leaves and Swords"!) "You will be hearing in due course what your next posting will be. For the time being you may consider yourself without one."

As I descended the steps with Galland he shot me a questioning look.

"Like you, *Herr General*—unemployed. No posting until further notice."

He was silent for a while. Then he growled, "And I'm not even allowed to move around freely—have to report where I am the whole time."

"Perhaps we're going to get away with it again," I said. "They can't silence all of us—or put us all in jail. You least of all!"

"Maybe we'll be lucky," was Galland's reply. "Fatty will never forgive you for having had the courage to tell him the truth. I'm the ringleader as far as he's concerned. He feels deeply humiliated. But his star is already so low in Hitler's eyes that he can't afford another mistake."

The task of dislocating the German oil resources had been completed and the remnants of the German Luftwaffe were grounded with empty tanks while unable to play any part in the closing stages of the German collapse.

The fighter crews were forced to sit idly by and watch Bomber Command and the American Air Force destroying German cities . . .

The account in establishing the final triumph of Bomber Command, the attack on Dresden of 13th and 14th February, is the requiem for the German Air Force.

Anthony Verrier
The Bomber Offensive
B. T. Batsford Ltd 1968

7
January–February 1945

After a week's leave in Greifswald, where I waited in vain for my transfer order, I returned to Berlin. I spent a further week at the Gatow guest barracks, but still nothing arrived about my new posting. I steered clear of the headquarters of the new General of Fighter Pilots, having on top of everything else a personal aversion to that ambitious and humorless man who—I believed—was in no way qualified to take over so responsible a post in a situation so serious. At breakfast in the officers' home I always tried to avoid the officers I knew, but it was only a few days before I was sitting on my own in any case. I felt like a stranger among all the new faces. Galland's men had all been ousted by the "wind of change" now blowing through the place. Göring had placed us under the "ban of the Reich"*—to use his own extraordinary expression.

It hurt to be ignored like that. Sometimes, during one of their overloud discussions, they would even forget that I was in the room. None of the "mutineers"—the people I could have opened my heart to—was reachable. Galland, after a week's house arrest, had left the capital; he was said to be with friends, indulging his one great passion—hunting. So little by little the plan took shape in my mind to go down to Italy to see Lützow. I should have known it would miscarry. Hauptmann K. "organized" a travel pass for me that or-

*"Reichsacht."

117

dered me to report to the *"Jagdfliegerführer Oberitalien"*—only by a somewhat unconventional route that took me via Kitzbühel, where I wanted to spend a few days skiing.

They were agony, those days in Kitzbühel—all I needed to have the last of my self-respect drained out of me. I stayed at the Luftwaffe Hotel, which at that time of year was packed with officers of all ranks in search of rest and relaxation. The weather was sunny and warm, the sky above the snow-covered mountains already held a hint of spring, and the hotel guests were doing their level best to shut the war out of their minds, lounging on deck chairs on the Hahnenkamm or at the foot of the runs, meeting one another in the bar or celebrating in their rooms, and always managing to conjure up from sources unknown large quantities of alcoholic refreshment.

I knew the Kitzbühel runs well, and I decided to earn the thrill of each descent by climbing the slope with furs attached to my skis. But always when I reached the peak around noon the same thing happened: the sonorous drone of heavy bombers made me search the sky to the south until I made out the countless vapor-trails of those mighty formations of Flying Fortresses. Every day almost on the dot—they might have been flying to a timetable—they cruised over our wintersporting paradise, heading I suppose for Munich, Regensburg, Augsburg, Nuremberg . . . I saw the pale blue fuselages against the darker, almost purple sky, and I watched the fighter escort as they swung gracefully to and fro above the bomber formation. The spectacle lasted nearly an hour, with a repeat performance in the opposite direction in the afternoon.

As they came back their formation flying was no longer so precise, either because fighters or flak had broken it up or because they felt as safe as if they had been in God's hand. Then the fighters usually flew exuberantly low, underneath the bombers, cutting all sorts of capers and visibly reveling in their supremacy in the air.

Getting up in the morning, I found I was already dreading the moment of first registering that roar of engines from the south. My uniformed fellow-skiers seemed to be watching me with nosy interest, and in their eyes I thought I could read the question: "What's he doing here, then, with his Oak Leaves and Swords?"

I began to feel ashamed of myself.

*   *   *

Early in February I packed my bags and set out to see Lützow.

It was on the Brenner that I first tasted again the immediacy of the war with its violence, destruction, and death. The army train reached the pass in the early afternoon. We had hours of endless waiting behind us, stopping and starting, standing in the darkness of tunnels, and creeping along at walking pace.

They were just clearing up what the morning air-raid had damaged, destroyed, and killed. The points had been hurriedly repaired. We had to change trains. Stretchers lined the platform, bearing the wounded and dead who had not made it to the shelter in time. The Brenner Pass was a favorite target with the Allied bombers—and a rewarding one, too, because raids on it severely upset the provisioning of our troops in Italy.

We sat in silence in the chilly compartment and longed for the moment when the train would start to move. MPs went through the carriages, checking people's papers. A staff sergeant stopped in the door of our compartment and saluted. He checked our marching orders and passes, subjected me to a brief scrutiny, and then left the carriage. Shortly afterward a major—steel helmet, "Military Police" armband, 0.8 at his belt, puffy, "desk-job" face—pushed open the sliding door and snarled, "Papers, please." He leafed quickly through my traveling companions' documents and then began to take an intense interest in my marching orders and my paybook. He made a note of something and finally left the compartment with a grunt.

I must admit, I did not have the cleanest conscience in the world—an out-of-work colonel of the Luftwaffe, heavily decorated, traveling to Italy by train for "talks with Oberst Lützow." Nevertheless, as the train pulled out of the station, confident that there would be no more difficulties now I gave way to my thoughts with intervals of either dozing or sleeping until we arrived in Verona some time around midnight.

As I walked down the platform with a heavy suitcase in each hand I became aware of two rather formidable-looking MPs marching along behind me. Waiting at the barrier in a most imposing get-up was a major, who saluted and greeted me with the words, "*Heil Hitler, Herr Oberst*, would you mind stepping into my office?"

Clearly etiquette made no provision for my being relieved of the burden of my suitcases. At any rate I was obliged to lug them along to his office myself and I was beginning to feel pretty bloody-minded.

Dropping them with a crash in front of the major's desk, I sank panting into a rickety wicker chair and threw my passes on the table with a brusque "Here are my papers."

He examined the documents carefully, leafed through my paybook, and gave an embarrassed cough. "*Herr Oberst*," he began, and I could tell he was finding the whole thing very difficult. "I'm afraid we can't allow you to continue your journey. Orders from General Ritter von P."

"What is this nonsense?" I asked. I nearly asked, "Who do you think you are to . . . ?" but thought better of it and said instead, "I want to speak to the general."

"Certainly, sir—but I wonder if, after midnight, that's going to be possible?"

"I don't give a damn—I want to speak to the general," I demanded stubbornly. Of course I had realized straight away that I was in a far from strong position. It was going to look very much as if I was on my way to hatch fresh plots with the exiled Oberst Lützow.

In the adjoining room an NCO set about trying to get himself connected with the general, exhausting his entire German–Italian repertoire from patient pleading to obscene threats in a nerve-racking battle with the idiosyncrasies of the Italian telephone system. He finally seemed to have made it; covering the mouthpiece with one hand he whispered, "It's the chief of staff—the general's not available."

I took the phone and said, "Steinhoff."

"Hallo, Steinhoff," came his honeyed voice. "What brings you to Italy?" He always opens like that, I reminded myself, and when you've fallen for it and start talking too much he suddenly tears a strip off you.

"I wish to discuss one or two questions regarding fighter operations with Lützow."

"On orders from whom?" he countered, and as he said it I knew he had me.

I had never been able to stand the man. For me he had always been the prototype of the ambitious, ruthless general-staff officer. As chief of the air fleet in Italy he had already made my life a burden once. Having in Richthofen an outstandingly forceful and capable superior, he had attempted to demonstrate an at least equal degree of toughness and nerve—with negative success.

It was in the autumn of 1943 that my group had to evacuate the airfields around Foggia. The front was getting swiftly closer as the

Allies pushed northward up the Adriatic coast. The air fleet chief of staff accordingly gave orders for one wing, together with the group staff, to transfer to Ciampino North airfield, near Rome. I protested and tried—unsuccessfully—to contact fleet HQ by telephone. The situation was becoming critical, however, so we took off, landing at Ciampino with an uneasy feeling that we were as good as handing ourselves to the Allied bombers on a plate. As soon as the wing was down I rang the air fleet chief of staff to complain bitterly about his—as I saw it—colossal blunder. It was nothing short of madness, I told him. Transferring a fully intact fighter wing unprotected to the largest airfield in the area, which every bomber pilot knew about, was tantamount to provocation. And I had no doubt that the Allies would finish us off.

"I must insist that my orders are carried out as received," he snapped. "I won't have you telling me what to do!" His German had taken on a hard Bavarian accent.

"Yes, sir," I said. What alternative did I have?

They wiped out my fighter wing two hours later. Like an enormous flat-iron they went twice over everything on the airfield that projected above ground level—hangars, buildings, aircraft, vehicles, and the people who had not managed to reach shelter. They laid a bomb carpet without a single hole in it; the entire wing was a write-off.

When I finally found a telephone that was still working and got through to fleet HQ I heard the chief of staff's voice say, "Ah, Steinhoff—what's the problem?"

It took my breath away. "Nothing in particular, sir—just to report that the first wing of Fighter Group 77 has ceased to exist. It and the group staff have been destroyed on the ground."

"Regrettable, Steinhoff, regrettable," was his prompt reaction. The catastrophe appeared to leave him unmoved.

"We've got large numbers of dead and wounded and barely an aircraft left intact," I burst out. Then, anger taking over, I yelled at him, "This is an irresponsible bloody shambles . . . !" But I got no further.

"Don't you talk to me like that!" he shouted back. "Where are your manners, man?" After a pause: "You'll report to me immediately." And then the crowning cynicism: "I must ask you not to dramatize so—after all, there's a war on."

"After all, there's a war on; after all, there's a war on . . ."—the words echoed in my ears as I drove back to my shattered wing. And my contempt for the man began to grow from that day on.

I was now required to tell him on whose orders I had come to discuss fighter-operations questions with Lützow. I could think of no one and in any case gave up the whole pretense then and there.

"I have no posting at the moment, *Herr General.*" (Yes, he had become a general in the meantime!) "I want to see my friend Lützow and have a talk with him."

There was a pause before he said firmly, "You have no orders to speak to the *Jagdfliegerführer Oberitalien.* You will return to Germany by the next train and report to the Head of Personnel, General M. Is that clear?"

"*Jawohl, Herr General.*"

The MP major said simply, "The next train for Munich leaves at four in the morning, sir. If you care to have a lie-down on the palliasse in the next room . . ."

I accepted gratefully, and just before four, still in pitch darkness, I climbed into an empty first-class compartment, stretched out on the seat, and covered myself with my leather greatcoat.

The first interruption came after Trento. It was already light when we pulled up with a squeal of brakes, the locomotive whistling and shrieking like a wild animal. Air-raid warning. I pulled my heavy suitcases down from the rack and joined the other field-grey figures on the embankment. Crunching through track ballast, I lugged those brutes of cases at a stumbling run toward the protection of a cave in the rock-wall of the cutting. Privates who were likewise hurrying along heavily laden with their leave or transfer luggage clearly got a tremendous kick out of ignoring the colonel staggering along with them practically on his knees. But I was already growing accustomed to being an out-of-work national hero. The weeks in no-man's-land, without privileges and without even existing—let alone being of any use—as far as the Luftwaffe was concerned, had lent me a detachment from things that had left me free and in a sense even happy.

When, squatting on one of my suitcases in the shelter of the cave, I drew out a case of excellent, mild Dutch cigars I was very soon surrounded by privates chattering almost on terms of equality with this curious bird they found wandering around without any kind of suite or ceremony. The attack failed to materialize and the locomotive whistled the all-clear. This time I got a little help with my suitcases—from volunteer porters all puffing on cigars.

The second interruption was more unpleasant. It occurred near Erlangen. I had slept, eaten some of my provisions (which at that time it was advisable to carry with one), and slept some more. As the train again pulled up with an incredible jerk in the middle of nowhere—it was around four in the afternoon—I heard the whine of fighter engines . . . Mustangs! I shot out of the compartment—without my bags this time—just as an MP came running along the corridor shouting, "No one's to leave the train, no one's to leave the train!" But I had already wrestled the window down and was shouting for my part, "Get out, get out—they'll shoot us to pieces!" A number of officers and men spilled out of the windows and doors behind me and made off. Looking back, I could see the steel-helmeted transport officer waving his pistol and shouting over and over again, "No one's to leave the train!"

It was rolling, open country. We had halted in the middle of a field between two bits of forest. Green shoots of winter corn poked up through the snow, and the broken soil was dark and wet. I was heading at a run for the nearest trees when the fighters swept over the field and opened up on the locomotive. Throwing ourselves flat, we waited until the air appeared to clear for a moment and then leapt up again and made it to the shelter of the trees. The fighters, escorting a big flight of bombers, were on their way home to England. The bombers had probably raided Regensburg or Nuremberg or some other city. The Allies had destroyed so much of the Reich already that they were running short of targets and occasionally just bombarded any old place. Now the fighters were picking up whatever "loot" offered itself on the homeward run. And locomotives and rolling stock were becoming increasingly popular targets with them.

As the Mustangs dived I counted five or six of them. After only one attack the locomotive disappeared in a white cloud, losing steam with a hiss. They then raked the train with machine-gun fire along its whole length, and we saw men running, throwing themselves flat, and getting up to run again.

After ten minutes it was all over. When I got back to the train I saw the transport officer dashing helplessly about looking for a doctor. He had been too late in deciding to evacuate the train, and now we had wounded and dead. We sat for hours and hours in the chilly train, until late in the evening they brought up another engine and we continued our journey toward the capital.

As the moment of our arrival at Anhalt Station drew nearer and nearer, I became more and more anxious about what would happen now. Undoubtedly Personnel would have been alerted and would be wondering what fresh mischief I might be cooking up with Lützow. Possibly they would even be waiting for me at the station.

But the train pulled into a deserted platform. It was raining bleakly. A swelling sea of pale faces, the passengers swept toward the barrier past the rapidly emptying train. Everyone seemed glad to have reached Berlin and was in a great hurry. I found a telephone and dialed Hauptmann K.'s number.

He answered the first ring. "Thank goodness you're back, sir. No one knew how to get hold of you. You're to phone General Galland immediately, if you will." He gave me the number and I got Galland straight away.

"Where've you been, man?"

"I tried to visit Franzl—without success. They caught me in Verona and sent me back on the next train. I'm to report to the Head of Personnel first thing."

"What a hare-brained idea, trying to go and see Lützow! Well, you needn't report to Personnel. If you want to do some flying, Macky, you can do it in the jet-fighter squadron we're setting up between us—OK?"

It knocked all the breath out of me. Here was I, expecting to be court-martialed, and Galland offered me the chance of flying in a squadron of jet fighters!

"Surprised you, did I?" Galland went on. "It's quite simple, really. Speer told Hitler about the failure of our plan. Hitler was furious and said he saw through the whole business. He asked Göring a couple of days ago what Galland and the mutineers were doing now. Göring told him the truth: that I was sitting around without a job. 'Well, then give him a chance to prove that this aircraft is a superior fighter,' Hitler told him. 'Give him a unit!'

"I was at Karinhall yesterday. Göring most ungraciously asked me whether I wanted to set up and command an experimental unit using jet aircraft. He suggested a squadron—the cheapest solution. I accepted."

"*Herr General*, I'm your man. When and where do we start?"

"Tomorrow morning—in Brandenburg."

The night of 13–14 February was clear and still. Dresden was packed with refugees. People were told to make for the air-raid shelters. In the Sarrasani Circus the announcement was made by the clowns, who accompanied it with a couple of gags . . . the fire took on cyclonic proportions, fed by the drop in pressure it had itself provoked—until the sky, more merciful than man, dropped torrents of rain to extinguish the flames. Defense was as impossible as flight. Those who stayed in the air-raid shelters suffocated. Those who came out were cremated in a sea of fire. The asphalt burnt in the streets. A crowd caught in the old market blazed like a forest. Hundreds of people, desperate to escape the agony of the flames, drowned in the River Elbe . . .

Translated from the French of
Raymond Cartier
La Seconde Guerre Mondiale
Paris 1965

8

Brandenburg
February 1945

It was my third posting in Brandenburg in five years of war. This time
it was not as the commander of a fighter group but rather as a kind
of "maid of all work," responsible, along with the OC, a lieutenant-
general, for putting together a squadron.

Why on earth did they spare the airfield? I wondered repeatedly.
They were blowing everything else to bits, including things that were
indubitably of lesser strategic importance than an airfield that had
become a branch of the aircraft industry and on which a weapon
was being forged that could come to represent a lethal danger to the
bombers.

The riddle remained unsolved: they must simply have overlooked us.

We threw ourselves into the task with the same spirit and enthusiasm that had characterized the early days of the Luftwaffe. We had
orders—or rather we had permission—to set up a squadron. Such a
unit would normally have been commanded by a first lieutenant or a
captain. It was regarded as the first step in the career of a young
officer on the way up, a position in which he could "prove himself."
But I was a colonel, with experience of commanding whole groups,
and my OC was a general whose face adorned postcards that were
sold in mass editions by enterprising profiteers sporting party badges.

The squadron we had permission to set up was admittedly a "jet-fighter squadron," an experiment that was to give us an opportunity of proving the truth of our contention that the Me 262 was a fighter and capable of shooting down bombers. But it was still only a squadron, i.e., in army terms a mere company. And ultimately it was only a "probationers' squadron," a unit for soldiers who had been ordered to the front on probation. A forlorn little troop of the outcast and condemned. Not that in our case we had been formally sentenced, but that was very much what it looked like.

"You can have anyone you want," Göring had told Galland. He had meant of course the "mutineers," because he had added, "You can have Steinhoff and Lützow right away."

My flat was on the ground floor of one of the officers' houses that lay under tall trees not far from the runway. It was a lieutenant's flat, consisting of one large room with bath. The army-issue furniture—three chairs, a table, and a bookcase, with the wardrobe out on the landing—was of pale stained beech. A blue worsted carpet with once-white spots lay on red linoleum. It was a nice, peacefully decorated lieutenant's flat that reminded me of the few years of peace I had enjoyed as a lieutenant. An inventory of the contents was thumb-tacked to the back of the door.

Yet most of those officers' flats—luxury apartments compared with some of the accommodation I had put up with at various fronts—now stood empty. Over the five years that the war had now lasted the inhabitants had changed almost weekly. And with the growing danger that the bombers would one day plough up the field, growing numbers of people had moved out. The surrounding villages and hamlets had been commandeered, people had billeted themselves on the local population, and the airfield's living-quarters were now virtually deserted.

Accommodation aside, the early days of "Fighter Unit 44," as we were called, were far from being days of plenty. Our transport, for example, consisted of a single jeep and my tiny 90 cc DKW motorcycle, which I had contrived to get assigned to us. My old unit, Fighter Group 7, was stationed on the same airfield, but they had orders from General Galland's successor not to lift a finger to help us. For the most part they just ignored us, though there was the occasional smile of condescending sympathy for the "mutineers." (One or two of my former comrades looked as if they had a sneaking admiration for us, but they were probably under pressure not to show it. The vast majority of those who saw us pottering about the airfield, training busily, thought we were quite simply mad.)

The general, however, had influential friends, and we soon found ourselves on the receiving end of a swelling supply of equipment, aircraft, spares, and weapons. We even got a second jeep. Fighter Group 7 asked for my motorbike back, so I buzzed cockily across to the taxiway on it and told them they could . . .

The pilots they reluctantly detached to us were young and inexperienced. An exception was Major "Bubi" Schnell, but we appropriated him ourselves without a transfer order on his release from hospital, where he had been recovering from a wound. (The once so celebrated Luftwaffe organization had come badly out of joint and now left many a loophole.) I became "Head of Training," and my faithful old "Kaczmarek" Fährmann we made technical officer, a job he had never done in his life before.

Leutnant Blomert came from the bombers. He was a Ju 88 specialist who had flown his last loop at flying school.

On the way out to the hardstand where the aircraft were parked I had a quick word with him. I explained that I wanted to fly to the eastern front—now only a short distance away—and that he should fly beside me, copying my every movement and hanging on like a leech.

As the jeep bowled along I remember wondering yet again why our airfield had escaped bombardment. They must have known we were assembling the jets there. They only had to knock out the hangars and the runways and we were finished. In fact it was tempting to see the whole arrangement as a further example of the incredible irresponsibility of the Luftwaffe leadership. But what other way was there of setting up a fighter unit and preparing it for action? When you have lost control of the air so completely as the German Luftwaffe had at that stage of the war, everything you do to try and win it back involves intolerable risk.

Beyond the hardstand where the new aircraft stood in rows was an area of shallow gravel pits, undergrowth, weeds, and rubbish tips. Climbing out of the jeep, we were startled by a loud whistling noise followed by a powerful detonation. Down in the first gravel pit ten or

Johannes Steinhoff as a baby, 1914.
Courtesy of Ursula Bird.

Steinhoff as a student, circa 1932–1934.
Courtesy of Ursula Bird.

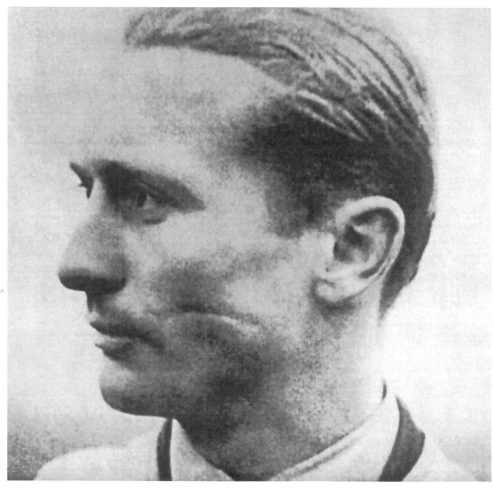

Steinhoff already sported a facial scar, but his plane crash in 1945 would make this pale in comparison. *Courtesy of Ursula Bird.*

This photo shows Steinhoff wearing his Ritterkreuz, or Knight's Cross, the throat decoration that formed the basis of the Nazi award system. *Courtesy of Ursula Bird.*

A German artist's wartime portrait of Steinhoff not only shows his Ritterkreuz with additional awards, but also the strain of several years of intense combat. *Courtesy of Ursula Bird.*

A German Me 109G-6 of II/JG 77 (foreground) flies formation with a Macchi 205V Veltro of the Aeronautica Nazionale Repubblicana (ANR) over the Alps in 1944. The ANR was formed after the fall of Benito Mussolini and continued to fight alongside the Germans. The Aeronautica Co-Belligerante (Co-Belligerant Air Force) fought with the Allies flying Allied aircraft. Although seldom a major factor in the air war, the Italians did field several attractive fighters, especially the Macchi 202/205 series, which, though lightly armed, gave very good accounts of themselves when flown by competent pilots. *Courtesy of John Weal.*

Possibly Steinhoff's Me 109G-2 while he was Gruppenkommandeur of II/JG 52 on the eastern front in the late summer of 1942. The "Gustav" was the definitive 109 model, although other variants followed. *Courtesy of John Weal.*

Shown wearing a flight jacket with sleeve rank markings of a Hauptmann (captain), Steinhoff leans against the windscreen of his Me 109. *Bundesarchiv, Koblenz.*

Steinhoff in the Mediterranean, mid-1943. Now an Oberstleutnant (lieutenant colonel) and a battle-tested leader of JG 77, he wears the Knight's Cross and Oak Leaves and has tallied some 150 of his eventual 176 kills. *Courtesy of Ursula Bird.*

Reichsmarschall Hermann Göring, himself a World War I ace with twenty-two kills and the *Pour le Mérite* (Germany's highest award of that period), visits the JG 2 "Richthofen" squadron at its base on the French coast in October 1940. On Göring's left is Maj. Helmut Wick, then the ranking Luftwaffe ace. Wick was killed the following month right after scoring his fifty-sixth victory. Steinhoff, then an Oberleutnant (first lieutenant), was assigned to JG 52 at another base along the same coast during the Battle of Britain, during which he scored six kills. *Courtesy of Ursula Bird.*

Johannes and Ursula in a wartime photo. *Courtesy of Ursula Bird.*

Johannes and Ursula's wedding day, April 29, 1939. *Courtesy of Ursula Bird.*

Me 262s on the JV 44 flight line at Brandenburg-Brest, 45 km west of Berlin. Adolf Galland chose a deceptively simple title for his squadron of *experten*. Jagdverband means only "fighter unit," while the "44" had several political inferences. JV 44 gained fifty-six kills in just two months. *EN Archives.*

"We were well on the way to becoming conspirators." Steinhoff (right) confers with Gunther Lützow. Both were now members of Adolf Galland's JV 44 in 1945. Galland had brought Steinhoff in as the unit's training officer. Lützow eventually had 108 kills before he himself was killed in action in late April 1945. *EN Archives*.

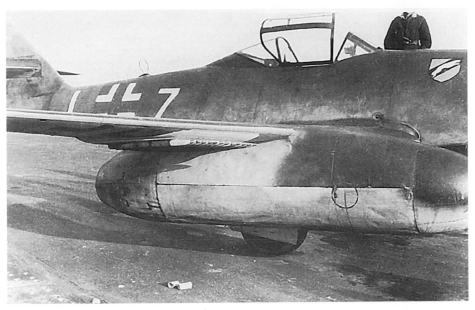

An Me 262A-1a of JG 7 carries R4M rockets below its wing. These early air-to-air missiles, twelve to a wing, were surprisingly effective during the war's last months. Some sixty Me 262s were modified to carry R4Ms, which were first used in combat on March 18, 1945. The JG 7 insignia has been alternatively described as a leaping greyhound or running fox. The shield is light blue with a black diagonal band. *EN Archives.*

An Me 262A-1a of JG 7 taxis toward the runway in February 1945. The black bars on either side of the fuselage cross denote the commanding officer's aircraft, while the red band on the rear fuselage indicates the aircraft is involved in home defense duties. *EN Archives.*

.An Me 262 of JG 7 takes off in early 1945. *EN Archives*.

After the crash. "[The doctor] . . . beat his hands together over his head the first time he saw me to take a look at my eyes." Steinhoff had to wear dark glasses to protect his eyes because he could not close them after the crash. In 1969, doctors made new eyelids from the skin of his forearm. *Courtesy of Ursula Bird*.

As the chief of staff of the West German Air Force, Steinhoff and Ursula receive guests. He held this position from 1966 to 1970. *Courtesy of Ursula Bird.*

In 1973 and now chairman of NATO's Military Committee, Steinhoff (far left) sits with Jules Léger, the Canadian ambassador to Belgium and Luxembourg. U.S. Secretary of State Henry Kissinger (second from right) engages former British Prime Minister Sir Douglas Hume. *Courtesy of Ursula Bird.*

At home with one of his canvases. Painting was one of Steinhoff's loves. *Courtesy of Ursula Bird.*

Ursula and Johannes celebrating his seventieth birthday, September 15, 1983. *Courtesy of Ursula Bird.*

so shapeless figures in blue boilersuits and pistol belts were firing rockets at large targets on which the outline of a tank had been painted in black. Certain of the figures—who clearly all belonged to a fairly advanced age group—were distinguished by the broadness of their behinds. On their heads they wore army skiing caps. Then I saw the woman—a matron of imposing proportions. Her fair hair was done up in a bun, which had the effect of pushing the peak of her skiing cap down over her eyes. She was waving her arms about energetically, and her throaty voice carried all the way to where we were standing.

I was having my first glimpse of Hitler's *Volkssturm*, the "People's Army" he had created a few weeks after telling me and my fellow-candidates for decoration the August before: "I shall mobilize the German nation in a way the world has never seen before." As I was preparing to climb into the cockpit of the world's fastest and most modern military aircraft, only a few yards away elderly citizens who had certainly never been soldiers were exercising with a rocket-launcher designed to destroy tanks at close quarters. Pale with fatigue, they offered a depressing spectacle. As if aware of the situation's macabre side, they hardly once glanced over in our direction. To them we must have seemed like representatives of a special, privileged class—as indeed we were. We were wearing the new grey leather outfits with the velvet collar. Our yellow silk scarves were knotted stylishly. Gloves, fur boots, pistol belts—everything was elegant and brand-new. The *Volkssturm* people in their baggy boilersuits must have wondered what to make of us. The propaganda machine had put us on a pedestal as "knights of the air" and heroes; possibly they forgave us our snobbishness in the belief that we could achieve miracles.

Our mechanics were busy with the aircraft and were taking no notice of the people in the gravel pit. Blomert stood beside me, looking pale and nervous. He was obviously keen to learn fighter flying, which was still a closed book to him.

"You release the brakes as soon as I lift my machine off and you see me retract my undercarriage. . . . We'll fly in tactical formation. Stay to port or starboard of me and keep enough distance between us. But don't whatever you do lose sight of me."

"Right, sir."

"We'll fly around Berlin to the north. As we approach the Oder we must expect to meet Russian fighters. So stick with me!"

"Right, sir."

I lifted my feet from the brakes and the aircraft slowly, ever so slowly, began to move. The thrust developed by the turbines was inadequate for so heavy an aircraft at the start. Then I began to pick up speed, rudder and elevators started responding to the stick and the foot pedals, and after a seemingly endless run the machine lifted off the ground. (It was the same in the air; the aircraft always seemed to take an age to get up the kind of speed that made combat maneuvers possible.)

Almost immediately Berlin spread out below us. The air was brightly transparent, although just above the enormous city a veil of mist lay like a sheet of frosted glass, giving the colors of its roofs, streets, and lakes a pale, filtered look. To the south, grey clouds billowing up out of this milky blue sea showed where the Mosquitoes had dropped their air mines in the night. We were looking at the capital of the Reich (though now it only came to life during the hours of daylight)—and a few flying minutes away the battle raged on the Oder.

I had been in Berlin two days before.

The depressing atmosphere of the beleaguered city hit me as soon as I stepped from the train. People eyed me as if I had been partly to blame for it all. My elegant tunic, leather-trimmed breeches, and riding-boots seemed out of place among the soldiers' beetle-crushers and knapsacks. The grey-faced civilians in threadbare winter coats took little or no notice of the colonel with the Knight's Cross, Oak Leaves, and Swords.

Stopping to look in a shop window—one that was still intact—I heard a vehicle screech to a halt at the curb behind me.

"Hello—the officer over there! Please put your gloves on."

They were very worried about the way discipline was slackening; desertion and malingering were on the increase, and the Wehrmacht was going rapidly downhill.

When I turned to face the MP patrol they froze in their seats, stammered out an apology, and drove off. But I felt neither satisfaction, nor pride, nor malicious pleasure at their embarrassment. The role of national hero was played out by now.

The uniformed lady at the ticket office bent down to get a better view of me through her little square window.

"Here, let's have a look . . . Knight's Cross with Swords, isn't it?"

"Yes."

Looking up at me through eyes that were wide with lack of sleep, she asked, "Are you still flying, then? Where is Hermann's Luftwaffe, anyway?"

I reached quickly for the ticket she had pushed out at me and murmured something like, "Certainly we're flying . . . only there are too many of them. . . ."

But the person behind had already pushed me away from the window. I hurried down the dark platform to my train.

We flew east along the dead-straight road leading from Berlin to Frankfurt-an-der-Oder. The landscape below us, with its great forests—leafless now, and black as a charcoal drawing—the occasional train with its long white plume of smoke, and the dots that were isolated farms and villages, conveyed an impression of innocent peace. But along the River Oder fires emitting dirty brown clouds of smoke marked where the front lay. I could trace the line of the river stretching endlessly away to the north, and all along it were these beacons of the battle of which the Wehrmacht bulletin spoke daily. Suddenly what looked like cottonwool balls—they were flak clouds—appeared in the air in front of us as if to bar our way. (Good gunners—the altitude was spot on!) We had crossed the Oder, and I began to lose height to get a better view of what was happening on the ground.

The Russian fighter appeared out of nowhere, the sharp black silhouette of his aircraft with its pointed wings becoming rapidly larger. Unprepared, I could not coordinate the movements of my Me 262 and line up my sight with the target in the seconds available. I shot past him uncomfortably close, climbing steeply into the deep blue sky. Looking back, I found myself staring straight into the fighter's cannon. He had pulled his aircraft into a vertical climb and was firing continuously.

You made a big mistake there, I thought to myself. You should have approached him from a position way below him, where he cannot see you. Then you should have pulled up at the last moment and let him have it in the fuselage from underneath.

Below me a whole swarm of fighters was circling, maybe ten or twelve of them. They were flying the kind of disorganized maneuvers—all abrupt turns, climbs, dives, loops, and spirals—that were a part of their tactics. There was an element of cocky exuberance in it too ("We're flying over the Reich—where are the famous German fighters?").

The temptation to get one of them in line with my sight was enormous. But as soon as they saw me they would start banking even more wildly, never flying straight for more than a few seconds at a time, and make my approach extremely problematical. I must withdraw until I was out of their field of vision and then approach them at their own altitude, taking them by surprise and relying on my speed to carry me through the whole circus. I should have to react very fast, picking off one that was flying straight and keeping my eyes open to avoid ramming any of the others.

Where was Blomert? I saw him far behind me, obviously having trouble keeping up. Could I risk it with him? But, as had happened hundreds of times before in this war, the still, small voice of caution was drowned by the overwhelming desire to "have a go," to snatch at the chance of getting to grips with the enemy. Throttle back carefully. Spiral down in a left-hand turn. Blomert was back in tow, below me to port. Out of the corner of my eye I saw the sun glint off the Russian fighter's plexiglass hood. Speed: 870 kph—too fast. Flatten out carefully. Where were the Russians? The sun was behind me now and would blind them as they tried to find me. Head forward slightly to get the right eye to the luminous sight. Index finger on the trigger on the front of the control stick. Blomert still in tow.

I could see them now, like black dots on the armored glass in front of me. Next second I was in the middle of their aerial ballet. I passed one that looked as if it was hanging motionless in the air ("I'm too fast!"). The one above me went into a steep right-hand turn, his pale blue underside standing out against the purple sky. Another banked right in front of the Me's nose. Violent jolt as I flew through his airscrew eddies. Maybe a wing's length away.

That one in the gentle left-hand curve! Swing her round. I was coming from underneath, eye glued to the sight ("Pull her tighter!"). A throbbing in the wings as my cannon pounded briefly. Missed him. Way behind his tail. It was exasperating. I would never be able to shoot one down like this. They were like a sack of fleas. A prick of doubt: is this really such a good fighter? Where was Blomert? Way behind me, a good 2,000 meters lower but trying to stay with me. What was I doing wrong? Could one in fact successfully attack a group of erratically banking fighters with the Me 262?

Still twenty-five minutes' flying time.

I must come at them from below, I decided. My speed would not be so great then, and who expected to be attacked from below? On the other hand they had now gone completely berserk. They had seen me flash through them like a shark, and they had no means of knowing that I was at a loss for a tactic to use against them. If only it were not so difficult to lose height without gaining too much speed. Pressure on the stick grew with my speed to such an extent that it required an enormous physical effort to bank the aircraft into position for a fresh attack. Actually it was unlikely that I would get one now. They knew that they were in danger from an aircraft that was phenomenally fast and they were now looping and spiraling about like mad. But they had also gained a great deal of self-confidence. They had penetrated deep into the Reich and were flying within sight of the capital. German fighters put in only a rare appearance, being almost exclusively engaged against the bomber streams flying in from the west.

My long banking turn had taken me back over the Oder and I was down to little more than 1,000 meters. Now I must climb to come up in the middle of the fighter swarm. Automatically registering that Blomert was in position, I pushed the throttle forward and stood the Me on its wing to change direction.

It was then that I spotted the shadows of Russian fighter-bombers hurrying west along the big main road. There were six or eight of them; I saw them quite distinctly despite their camouflage. They were firing their cannon and dropping bombs. Here was a worthwhile target, and our ground troops needed to be relieved.

"Blomert, round to starboard, follow me. . . ."

Blomert appeared to be making a supreme effort to keep in position as I dived into a steep left-hand turn. This was his first contact with the enemy, and he was surely thinking, "For God's sake, what's he up to now?" The Russians were skimming along the road with cannon hammering. I could see a convoy of Wehrmacht vehicles, mostly trucks, stopping or turning off into side roads. Soldiers went scurrying off across the fields or threw themselves flat on their faces.

Here and there black clouds of smoke indicated hits. As I bent forward to look through the sight I noticed that I had too much speed again. The trees and fields were flashing past beneath me and the shape of the last fighter-bomber loomed alarmingly in the sight. ("Aim the luminous spot in the center of the sight at the middle of his fuselage, press the trigger by squeezing your hand round the stick, then pull the stick back sharply to avoid a collision.") The burst of fire was very short. The Stormovich started leaving a trail just as I pulled up over it, the tips of the tall pines almost seeming to brush the Me's wings. I had a great deal of speed now and the hard gusts of the east wind near the ground gave me a bad buffeting. I tried to keep an eye on the Stormovich over my left shoulder and heard myself groan as the acceleration laid its crushing weight on my shoulders in the turn.

The fighter-bomber hit the ground not far from the edge of the forest, first with its airscrew, then bouncing along on its belly throwing up a gigantic fountain of powdery snow. It came to an abrupt halt, the wind blew the snow away, and I saw the aircraft silhouetted against the white background and a black figure that emerged from the fuselage at that moment jumped down from the wing, and started leaping through the drifts toward the nearest trees. Pulling round in a wide turn over the wreck, I watched the fleeing figure disappear into the shelter of the dark forest. I remembered seeing a friend run for his life near Novgorod in exactly similar circumstances—except that that had been in the summer of 1941, the year of the victorious advance.

Blomert was still having trouble keeping up, and on the way back he told me he was running short of fuel. We reached Brandenburg on the last of our reserve.

We busied ourselves with the thousand and one trivial things that nevertheless have to be done if a squadron organized from scratch is to become a combat instrument. At the same time the work was therapy against thinking too much and against a growing feeling of being pariahs. The tiny unit stuck close together right from the start. Everyone knew that the high-ups did not trust us, that we were on trial, as it were, but also that no one would shed any tears if the unit and ourselves should cease to exist.

Toward the end of March the general began thinking about moving the squadron down south to Bavaria—"to protect what was left of the aircraft industry," as he put it. There was a growing danger that the Soviets and Anglo-Saxons, both thrusting toward Berlin, would cut the remaining pocket of resistance in two. And we had no wish to watch from the vicinity of the capital as Germany's fate was sealed.

His friends must have been influential indeed because at the beginning of April we began to make preparations for transferring to southern Germany. Although the unit had only just come into existence it was a full-sized goods train that eventually pulled out of the station loaded with technical equipment, spare turbines, armaments, tractors, vehicles—in a word, everything we had succeeded in getting out of the depots in that short time.

Two days later I followed with the flying unit, consisting of twelve jet fighters. I had waited for good weather in order to be sure of reaching Munich-Riem—our new base—nonstop, because there were not many fields with the kerosene we needed for our turbines. When we took off in the morning the weather was exactly as the previous evening's forecast had said it would be. Because it was still early we did not expect to meet any American fighters on the way, but if they had also made a very early start we might encounter some over Munich-Riem as we arrived, so we knew we must be on our guard.

That flight of less than an hour from Brandenburg to Munich was an experience I shall never forget. I was in excellent spirits, feeling as though I had escaped fate's clutches yet again, although I was perfectly aware that the Reich's days were numbered. But we were in the process of removing ourselves from the reach of the leadership, and as if we sensed that our tiny unit was the Luftwaffe's last remaining combat force, that we were in effect *the* Luftwaffe, the will to fight, to "show what we could do," had flared to life in us once more.

The clouds were hanging low over the southern Harz hills as we flew over my home, the lovely valley known as the "Golden Lea" (*die Goldene Aue*) north of the Kyffhäuser ridge. And when we came to the Thuringian Forest range farther south we had no more than 100 meters through which to slip between the peaks and the dark underside of the solid cloud layer.

The landscape lay peaceful and innocent-looking in the first green of spring. The forests and fields and villages slipped away beneath us as we cruised at more than 800 kph across into Upper Franconia. Lichtenfels, Schloss Banz, Vierzehnheiligen—where I had traced with my newlywed bride the poet Scheffel's footsteps. Erlangen, Nuremberg, Ingolstadt . . .

Munich.

There were no fighter aircraft in the Royal or United States Air Forces which could match the jets in performance. If any of the types had been produced in quantity there is little doubt that they would have destroyed many hundreds of British and American bombers.

Anthony Verrier
The Bomber Offensive
B. T. Batsford Ltd 1968

9
Munich-Riem
Early April 1945

When the alarm clock shrilled I had trouble resisting the temptation to stay in bed, because it was not until toward morning that I had fallen exhausted into a shallow sleep. My window looked east, and the trees and houses were already sharply silhouetted against the blue-grey morning sky. A cloudless sky. We would be flying—because the bombers would come, as they did every day—in two or three hours' time.

Slipping into the leather trousers, I pulled down the broad zip fasteners that closed the legs snugly round the ankles of my fur boots. The leather jacket with its plush lining was shapeless and heavy, but it kept out the dawn chill. Then I slung my pistol belt round my hips ("What for, actually?"). Today we wanted to experiment with firing rockets at the bombers. Fährmann would be flying with me.

In Riem there was—for the first time during the war—no officers' mess (not that in other places the accommodation—sometimes only a tent—had always been up to the traditional splendor of that institution). Very soon the various messes became simply pilots' canteens in which differences of rank tended to become increasingly blurred. It was clear to everyone that this airfield would be the end of the road as far as we were concerned, but even so we never began to fall apart

as a community. We talked together as we had always done throughout the past five years, cracking the old, superficial jokes in a jargon
that the profession of flying had molded and the war had made coarse
and cynical. We postponed any serious discussion about "after the
war" indefinitely, yet each of us began to develop his own ideas about
surrender, POW camp, and interrogation.

When we had arrived in Munich-Riem from Brandenburg the airfield commandant had arranged private accommodation for the pilots, there being no garrison in the vicinity (with the exception of the
SS riding school, to which we shall be coming back).

We were billeted on an innkeeper and his wife who unenthusiasti-
cally (they were polite one day and sullen the next) indicated their
acceptance of this—as they must have suspected—last military intrusion by preferring the greeting "*Grüss Gott*" to "*Heil Hitler*" and by
leaving us alone. Since our billets were scattered about the surrounding villages at some distance from the airfield we were obliged to get
up before sunrise and make our way in on bicycles, motorcycles, or
cars fitted with wood-gas converters. Mustangs and Lightnings would
appear over the field very early in the day, so that we were usually on
the alert in the dawn twilight. Only fog or low-lying cloud prompted
some to risk turning over again in bed, but they would all be at the
field in time if the weather cleared up sufficiently for us to fly.

Seldom can there have been a body of young men in which everyone
knew so much about everyone else. The general, who commanded the
little unit, was the idol of the Jagdwaffe. You could buy postcards of
him, you saw him at the cinema when they showed the news, and you
could read in the penny magazines devoted to the heroes of the war
how he had been keen on hunting* even as a small boy and how later
he and Mölders, who was the same age, had competed to see who
could shoot down the most enemy aircraft. People forgave him his
extravagance—the impossibly deformed caps, the tunic closed high at
the neck (he wore his Knight's Cross below the collar where it was at
its most decorative against the blue of his tunic), and the black cigars
that he only rarely removed from his mouth. The fact that the ladies
found him irresistible and that he was prompt to reciprocate the at-

---

Die Jagd. As many passages in this book show, the association between *die Jagd*
and *die Jagdwaffe* is not "merely" verbal (*Tr.*).

tentions of many a film and society beauty, rather than provoking our prudish indignation tended to earn him our respect—an attitude that was not shared by the phony puritans of the higher levels of the Luftwaffe leadership.

Other members of the squadron—notably Erich Hohagen (of the plexiglass skull) and Major "The Count" Krupinski—we salvaged from the "end of the world" atmosphere of the Fighter Pilots' Rest Home, a villa on the shores of the Tegernsee, south of Munich. This institution, intended as a place where battle-weary pilots could recuperate from the stresses of service at the front, had become a kind of club for those fighter pilots who preferred to enjoy their few days' relaxation with friends rather than with their families in the steadily more oppressive atmosphere of the "home front." During the course of the war a completely illusory world had taken shape here, a world in which all talk was of "the front" and one evaded the depressing realities of day-to-day life in the Reich. A world, too, that had "everything"—brandy, champagne, and various culinary delicacies. One celebrated one's engagement or marriage there, and one made appointments with friends. But over the years the ranks had thinned. New faces had appeared, new "heroes." The names of the fallen were the object of respectful murmurs at the bar. And now there was fear in the air, fear of the inescapable end.

When we arrived there—with still one day to go before we must be technically ready for action against the *Viermots*—we had no idea that we would find there the cream of the Luftwaffe's remaining fighter pilots. It was late afternoon when our wood-gas car pulled up at the garden gate. The general walked ahead up the drive, and when he opened the front door there was already a babble of voices coming from the bar. We pushed our way through the gloomy hall and had some trouble opening the door to the bar, so dense was the crowd around the bar counter in the tiny room.

". . . on the very threshold of victory the German people will not capitulate to the imperialists but will with the aid of the greatest popular uprising of all time, brought about by such a mobilization as history has never seen before, by the *Volkssturm* . . ."

The Goebbels imitator standing on a table with his tunic open broke off at this point, stared at the general open-mouthed for several seconds, then fluently pursued his improvisation in Goebbels's thick Rhenish accent: ". . . with the General of Fighter Pilots at its head . . ."

Unseen hands yanked the speaker off the table and everyone in the room stared at us in silence. Truly an astonishing company of Germany's once feared and fabled fighter pilots. I spotted Krupinski, whom I had not seen since my transfer from Russia to Africa in the spring of 1943. He struck me as more masculine now, more mature, no longer the soft young schoolboy. His chin, particularly, had developed, giving his face a tough, almost ruthless look.

"Enough of that nonsense," said the general, addressing the whole room. And as if this had been a signal, almost as if he had told them, "Look, I'm one of you," the babble of voices immediately resumed. They pressed round us, and before we knew what was happening we were leaning at the bar with glasses in our hands.

"What are you all doing here, actually, count?"

"Waiting till the show's over, sir," he said, his eyes glued to a table in the corner from which came the sound of female laughter.

He had been transferred to my squadron during the battle for England—an eighteen-year-old cadet officer, brazen-faced and cheeky, with no great talent for fighter flying. The result was that he found it difficult to keep pace with his year and accomplish what was expected of fighter pilots, namely shooting down enemy aircraft. When we were posted to the east the count was still the wallflower of my squadron, still completely useless as a fighter pilot, and I was thinking of turning him over to a reconnaissance or bomber unit. Then, one day, he suddenly found out how it was done.

It was in August 1942. We were stationed at an airfield on the outskirts of Maykop to provide fighter cover for the mountain infantry who were trying to thrust through the Caucasus jungle to the Black Sea. One morning we were flying low along the Black Sea coast where the tree-covered mountains rise straight up out of the sea. In a narrow valley one of my pilots spotted an airstrip on which a number of Ratas, those small fighter aircraft with the large radial engine and the stubby wings, were taxiing toward the runway for takeoff.

"Attention, Ratas in the valley to port . . ."

I immediately pulled my Me into a steep, tight turn, and just as I noticed the dust cloud that the Soviet fighters raised with their airscrews we flew into a web of red and white tracer bullets. The field, a long and very narrow one of the kind we used to call a "towel," was protected by heavy flak. The Ratas were just starting as we came swinging down. It was not particularly pleasant, hurtling over the treetops toward the runway through a thick curtain of flak. To make matters worse I heard a pilot report: ". . . hit by flak . . . losing coolant . . . flying home." Head laid right back, I took in the scene in the valley far below. Suddenly I saw a Me come shooting over the treetops at the end of the field and fly low along the runway—so low that its airscrew appeared to be brushing the ground. The flak gunners could hardly fire at it without endangering their own aircraft parked in the splinter boxes. At the end of the runway the Me pulled up sharply round a rocky ridge and was sitting behind a Rata that was trying to dive back into the flak-protected valley. At a burst of fire from the attacker it turned into a red ball and blew up. The author of the daredevil attack had been the count, and from that day on he appeared to have gotten the hang of it. Before long he was one of the stars of the Jagdwaffe.

"Count, you ought to be doing something more sensible than boozing here."

"It's the most sensible occupation I can think of at the moment, sir."

"How about joining our circus and flying with us?"

He stared at me, and it was a moment before he could speak.

"What—not the Me 262?"

"Certainly. We're looking for a few more experts."

"Right away, sir. Barkhorn's here too—he's sure to be interested."

"Report to us tomorrow morning if you can make it. You can bring Barkhorn with you. We've got enough aircraft. They're just dumping them on the airfield for us on the assumption that we can do something with them. The bombers, I mean, who were given priority on them before. You don't need a transfer order or anything like that. I'll tell you how to fly it—and then you'll be a pilot, nothing but a pilot. But you'll have to make it snappy."

The count came and so did Barkhorn. And not long afterward Lützow joined us from his Italian exile. I adopted a fairly informal approach to conversion training on the Me 262, feeling that time was running short and wanting to make it easy for the veterans. We had no instruction manuals or visual aids and the lessons were held in the open air with all of us squatting on the earthworks that had been thrown up round the jets. Or we sat on plain wooden benches near the telephone, on the alert, and I explained how one flew the Me 262. I told them what to do in order to fly it correctly—and what they absolutely must not do. I spoke of the aircraft's weaknesses, how it was very slow to gain momentum, jolting along the grass for an apparently endless length of time before one could risk pulling the stick back, and then only very, very carefully because an angle of incidence of one or two degrees sufficed to provide enough lift and because too steep an angle, caused by pulling too sharply on the stick, could kill one's speed—and with it oneself. I spoke of the phenomena of flight at speeds that none of them had flown before. How at high altitudes one should avoid touching the throttle at all if possible. How abrupt movements could cause explosions in the power plant, heralded by a sudden increase in engine noise. And I warned against over-steep gliding or diving at high altitudes since this could cause the ailerons to lose their effect without warning or even to have the reverse effect.

They had a thousand and one questions, and I spent hours answering them. Some of them only wanted to know exactly how to start and land, how much speed the gauge must show on takeoff, and what was the safest approach speed for landing. They were the born fliers. Others—and Franzl was one of them—pestered me repeatedly with the same questions. He would sit on the parachute and I would perch on the rim of the cockpit explaining the same things over and over again.

"What happens when I press this button? What must I do when the temperature of an engine goes above eight hundred degrees? When can I raise the undercarriage? What do I . . . ?"

Since there was no end to his questions I decided to let him start flying, hoping that this would help him overcome his fear of all the terrible things that might happen. The remedy was successful. He flew the aircraft and came back full of enthusiasm—as well as with a host of new questions, to most of which I had no answer. The other veterans climbed into the Me 262 without any hesitation, flew it to perfection, and were ready for action after only a few flights.

I burst out of the cloud cover into painfully bright sunlight and had to lean forward in the cockpit to see my instruments: 6,000 meters. The Alps lay before me in all their splendor, a chain of snow-capped peaks stretching as far as the eye could see, and beyond the peaks and ridges fog-filled valleys looked like enormous lakes.

Fährmann was flying behind me to port in the regulation position that would prevent us from colliding in the event of abrupt maneuvers. We had taken off to meet and attack a bomber formation that was flying in advance of a larger formation coming in over France from England. Their goal might be Munich, Nuremberg, or Regensburg. There was not a lot left to destroy; the Americans had almost reached Augsburg, and in the north they had already taken Würzburg and Kitzingen.

"Pantechnicons over Stuttgart, lots of them, heading for Munich." Ground control came through loud and clear—no interference.

I started a wide left-hand turn, handling the controls of the sensitive, high-speed aircraft carefully in order not to lose any of its momentum. The engines were humming evenly and without vibration. Just at that moment a swarm of Lightnings—American twin-boom fighters—shot across beneath us.

I have always wondered whether it was man's aggressive disposition to hunt that triggered one's reflexes so swiftly and immediately or whether it was the experience gained in a hundred dogfights that prompted one to make the right decisions in a fraction of a second— whether in defense or in attack. Undoubtedly the state of extreme tension was partly responsible for that reflex reaction, as well as the fact that years of practice at sneaking up on the enemy, dodging out of his way, and hiding in the infinity of the sky had developed new and unknown instincts in the few who had survived.

With a shout of "Lightnings down to port!" I found myself in a steep curving climb, partly in order to avoid the possibility of any others that might be above us taking us by surprise and partly to get into position to attack. Fährmann had tried in vain to stay with me and was now hopelessly left behind some 1,000 meters below, undoubtedly looking all over the place for me. I had to be quick. The Lightnings, standing out like toy aircraft against the dark cloud below them, were flying in neat formation on a northerly course, possibly to attack our airfield. They seemed to be in high spirits; every now and then one or other of them would stand his aircraft gracefully on one wingtip before dancing back to his place in the formation.

It all happened very fast. I could not worry about Fährmann; I had so much excess speed (and was gaining more the longer I dived) that I had my hands full looking after myself. The safety catch on my weapons had to be released. I unfastened the reflex sight—a luminous area on the windshield in front of me—and it promptly began to wander all over the place. We were trying for the first time to fire with a gyroscopic sight that allowed for lead and obliged the pilot to line the sight up with the target (the system was a failure because the technology of it was still imperfect). Then the Lightnings loomed up terrifyingly fast in front of me, and it was only for the space of seconds that I was able to get into firing position behind one of the machines on the outside of the formation. And as if they had received prior warning they swung round smartly as soon as I opened fire. Pop, pop, pop, went my cannon in furious succession. I tried to follow a Lightning's tight turn but the gravity pressed me down on my parachute with such force that I had trouble keeping my head in position to line the sight up with him. The sight was still wandering all over the windscreen and I shot too short; I thought I could see the acceleration drag the bullets down to pass harmlessly well below the Lightning's fuselages. Then a shudder went through my aircraft as my leading-edge flaps sprang out: I had exceeded the permissible gravity load.

The Lightnings made for the ground in tight spirals. No use trying to follow them: the Me 262 had no dive brakes. It was agony every time, losing height without picking up so much speed that the aircraft became uncontrollable.

"Danube One, are you in combat? Come in, Danube One . . ." Ground control had heard of course that I had spotted Lightnings, and anyway they were probably following my progress on their radar screen.

"Was in combat with Lightnings—no success."

"Victor," answered ground control. "Pantechnicons approaching Regensburg. How are you for juice?"

"About another thirty minutes," I replied.

"Fly on 100 degrees."

"Victor."

Where had Fährmann got to? I realized I had lost a lot of height. If I climbed through the thin cloud cover now I might still be able to attack the bombers. There were tiny patches of blue sky visible through the stratus layer—room enough to slip through. I did not fancy the idea of instrument-flying the Me 262 in cloud for any length of time. What little experience we had of flying the aircraft on instruments was not particularly promising.

I flattened out above the cloud cover at 8,000 meters to find Fährmann suddenly back beside me. He rocked his wings; evidently he was having radio trouble. If we did not meet up with the bombers in the next fifteen minutes we should have to turn back. The cloud cover, a harsh white in the bright sun, stretched away endlessly into the distance.

"Danube One calling. Please give position of pantechnicons."

"Fly on 60."

I ought to have been able to see them by now. The cloud cover made an ideal background, against which the formation would stand out clearly.

"Danube One, you should be running into pantechnicons now."

The formation of four-engined bombers was cruising along like a fly-past. They were pulling long vapor trails behind them, and the shadows of the trails lay like the lines of an exercise book on the glaring white cloud below.

"Danube has made contact."

Our superior speed took us across the tip of the bomber formation. I pulled my aircraft round to get an idea of the size of the formation, and before I knew what was going on I was shooting through a whole swarm of American fighters, completely incapable of reacting in any way. They were as surprised as I was and scattered in panic, some of them nose-diving to safety, others heaving their aircraft round in a series of wild banking turns.

("You must try and fly a classical attack, slipping into a space between flights and approaching from underneath—no problem with your speed plus—and you must get to within exactly 1,000 meters before firing the rockets. Otherwise you'll shoot too short and your whole approach will have been wasted.")

I had ten minutes left at most, but I had no idea how far I was from Riem airfield. The bombers were approaching Regensburg, however, so from 8,000 meters Riem must be reachable in only a few minutes. I hoped the Lightnings would not be watching the airfield as I came down, because a landing Me 262 was a helpless prey to any attacker.

The first and second flights were Liberators. Two other flights followed at some distance but I could not make out the type of aircraft. I calculated that if I pulled round now and lost my 1,000 meters of extra altitude, this would bring me into the best position for an attack.

"I'm attacking to starboard."

No answer from Fährmann, who followed in tight combat formation as I put the Me's nose down and my speed began to increase. I dived through the vapor trails and on for another few hundred meters until, seeing the bombers right above me, I pulled my machine up into their wake. I regarded the American fighters as harmless and ignored them; after all I was flying nearly twice their speed.

The inadequacy of our experience of aerial combat at high altitudes came home to me as the pressures on the Me's control stick grew. Warnings flashed through my head—"Fly no faster than 870 kph," "Careful not to touch the throttle," "Don't change your revs or the engines may blow up"—as I tried to keep the bombers in view. They were like so many spiders drawing their vapor-trail threads across the grey-blue sky. My leading-edge flaps sprang out as I pulled up sharply and began to climb. ("You must pull back the throttle"— which at that altitude could be fatal!) The colossal acceleration carried me right into the vapor trails ("A little bit more—careful of negative acceleration") and suddenly the tall tail sections of the Fortresses filled my windshield like a row of shark fins. When the bomber filled the circle of my luminous reflex sight, when its wingtips exactly touched the outer edge of the circle—that was the moment to fire the rockets. I would then be the requisite 1,000 meters from my target. Those few seconds of extreme concentration seemed endless. As the airscrew eddies shook my aircraft I activated the rockets: "Switch on red, aim at the middle of the trio of Liberators, and keep the Me as steady as you can!" As the Viermot floated up and down in my sight I saw out of the corner of my eye lines of red tracer bullets reaching out for me like long fingers. I clamped my right hand round the stick and pressed the release button.

Nothing happened! The rockets failed to ignite! ("Switch quickly to your cannon.") The glance down into the cockpit had cost me at least 100 meters of altitude. I was now lower than the bomber formation and my speed plus was enormous. I pulled up slightly, a Liberator floated through my sight, and the cannon spat a two- or three-second burst. My speed swung me up 2,000 or 3,000 meters above the bombers and I saw the Liberator I had attacked leaving a dark trail behind him. A hit!

The bomber formation continued on its way unperturbed, the next flight following about a kilometer behind.

"Danube One, my horse is lame."* Fährmann's voice sounded faint in my headphone.

*Luftwaffe code for "I have engine trouble" (J.S.).

"Are you in tow? Can you see me?" I must try and get him home. We had a maximum of ten minutes' flying time left. There was no answer so I called again and banked a few times to scan the air space behind me.

"Danube, I'm being attacked by fighters . . ."

He's had it now, I thought. I could not even give him any advice. He would defend himself as best he could. Perhaps he would dive into the clouds, or he might bale out.

"Danube Two, can you still hear me, Danube Two . . . ?"

No answer. Instead I got ground control:

"Danube One, fly on 235 degrees. Airfield is free."

I landed on my last fuel reserve. The squadron was preparing to take off against the main body of the bombers. Aircraft were taxiing with engines howling, mechanics dashed about busily, and trucks full of rockets and ammunition were bouncing over the grass.

"Where's Leutnant Fährmann?" asked the mechanic as I opened the cockpit. It was the old, anxious question when only one of a group of two landed.

". . . had engine trouble and was attacked by fighters . . ."

They asked no more, beginning to strip the plates from the cowling and loosen the tank cap, as they did after every mission. It was routine, and most of them had been at it for five years already. They had done the round trip to the limits of the Pan-German Reich, and now like me they had reached the end of the road. Like me, too, they must have seen the senselessness of what we were doing, because I noticed them whispering together and shaking their heads as they jogged off to their shelter.

Fährmann kept sending the distress call over and over again until he realized how useless it was. Who could do anything for him now? Looking out along the wing he saw a hole as big as a fish, edged with torn, distorted aluminum sheeting. The bullet had evidently hit the starboard turbine, because this was producing no more thrust.

He had lost a great deal of speed and, well aware of the danger, began to scan the air space for fighters. ("I won't make it to Riem! But she still flies. . . . Maybe I can find a big field, or I'll have to bale out. . . .")

So far only one or two pilots had baled out of the Me 262, and Fährmann knew that it was an extremely risky undertaking. "You're simply sucked out," said some, while others reckoned, "You lay the aircraft on its back and press the stick forward." But there was one thing Fährmann knew for a certainty, and that was that baling out of such a fast aircraft at low altitudes, where the air is thicker, was like smashing into a brick wall.

The black dots in the cruelly bright sky above him were Thunderbolts. The realization went through him like an electric shock, and while his mouth went dry and his heart began to beat wildly the salt sweat ran out from beneath his helmet and stung his eyes. The Thunderbolts—American fighters we feared because of their extraordinary ability to attack in a nose dive—had spotted an easy prey, and as they promptly pointed their noses to the ground Fährmann tried to get his crippled aircraft into the shelter of the cloud cover that spread out below him. He flew at high speed into the thin, yellowish veils of mist and realized immediately that his hope of escaping from the pack had been in vain. He was down to a couple of hundred meters when the tracer bullets began reaching for him from behind.

It all happened very fast. His cockpit was lit by a sudden flash as an incendiary bullet exploded just by his head. He registered a searing pain in the back of his neck, was aware of fields whipping past beneath him, and then he saw the row of giant poplars looming up at him.

Later he no longer remembered whether he had managed to pull the aircraft's nose up again, but his hands had worked with the speed of lightning. "Belt off, canopy away . . ." What he did remember was the appalling impact of the wall of air, like colliding with a solid mass. It forced his mouth wide open, wrenched his arms and legs all over the place, and sent earth and sky spinning dizzily round him.

Then came the brutal correction of this state of affairs by the jerk of the straps threatening to tear his thighs from their sockets as the parachute opened. The tall poplars came rushing toward him, his chute snagged in the branches and his body, after dangling violently to and fro several times on the end of the cords, came to rest against the mighty trunk only a meter from the ground. Straight in front of him, where the river made a bend, he saw a fountain of muddy water go shooting skyward. Immediately afterward the blast of a muffled explosion reached his ears. His Me had crashed into the Danube.

At the sound of men's voices he opened his eyes. Hanging in his parachute straps completely numb with shock, he had given himself up to the unreal-seeming silence with eyes closed. Still deprived of his sense of balance, he thought he was spinning round and round with diminishing speed until, after a long moment, a wave of pain washed through his whole body. He felt as if his arms and legs had literally been torn off.

The men were hurrying across the meadow toward him, waving their arms. He heard scraps of Bavarian dialect and thought he caught the words "*Ami*" and "*Engländer.*" When they were within a few paces of him he shouted, "I'm German!" They pulled up in their tracks, started asking the most inane questions as "Been shot down, then?" and "Got you, did they?"—and set about trying to free him from his predicament by tugging on his legs.

"Stop it, don't touch me—I ache all over!" he screamed. He was able to persuade them to support him very carefully with their shoulders and arms while another man released the catch of the parachute. The straps sprang away from his shoulders and thighs, and they lowered him gently to the ground.

At the cost of an enormous effort and with a man supporting him on either side he managed to make it to the nearest farmhouse. The farmer's wife tucked him straight up in the big double bed, and he fell asleep to the smell of frying eggs.

A gentle touch on his shoulder woke him up: "I'm the mayor of Lohhausen. I'm an auxiliary policeman too!"

Fährmann felt better, and for the first time since the bale-out he experienced a rush of happiness: "I'm alive!" Immediately active again, he sat up in bed and asked, "Please ring Munich-Riem for me—the phone number of my unit is such and such. I'm Leutnant Fährmann. Ask them to send a car."

The mayor nodded and made a note of the number.

"How long will it take a car to get here?" Fährmann asked.

"Be a good four hours with the roads what they are . . ."

From the kitchen came the rattle of coffee cups accompanied by a murmur of voices ("Isn't he young!"). He managed to stand up and walk as far as the sofa. They told him he would have to go a long way round because the bridges had been blown up. Also the SS were out looking for deserters ("And short work they make of them, too!"). The mayor had gone off to telephone, having promised to make out a certificate "to say that you're Leutnant Fährmann who's been shot down . . ."

Hours passed. Fährmann was dozing on the bed, beginning with the help of several shots of home-distilled schnapps to forget the pain he was in, when around midnight a fearsome-looking figure (steel helmet, face scarf, motorcycle coat, gas mask, pistol) blundered into the room.

"Gefreiter Müller reporting with the combination to pick up Leutnant Fährmann."

"For goodness' sake," said Fährmann. "How am I supposed to survive the journey in a sidecar?"

"It was the only vehicle available, sir."

When they went out to inspect the sidecar they made the discovery that instead of an upholstered seat it contained a battered tool box. The farmer's wife came hurrying with an armful of empty sacks, and onto these Fährmann, supported by two helpers, lowered himself with a groan. They wrapped a blanket round his shoulders, and since he had no cap the farmer's wife tied a brightly colored scarf round his head, knotting it under the chin.

It was a moving farewell. ("Mind how you go, then.") But the drive along bumpy field tracks was agony for Fährmann.

Dawn was breaking as they approached a roadblock before a bridge and a guard stepped out in front of the motorcycle to shout, "Stop! Dismount immediately! Are you out of your mind—gallivanting about the place on a Wehrmacht motorbike with a girl in the sidecar? Get out, you!"

Fährmann was too done up to be really angry. Tearing off the headscarf, he drew the mayor's certificate from his breast pocket and summoned almost his last strength to say: "Here—read this and let us through. I've had all I can take. . . ."

It was after sunup when he arrived back at the field; we were just getting ready to take off against the first bombers. Two days later he was taking off beside me again—on what was to be my last flight. . . .

The Allies seemed out to break all remaining resistance by bombarding the cities of what was left of the Reich without a pause, while the Russians mounted their final offensive against Berlin. At the usual early hour we took off for our next mission.

Our formation reached combat altitude after an endless climb just as the bomber stream crossed the Munich city limits. We had managed to get a proud total of nine jet fighters into the air at once, and suspended beneath each of those nine pairs of wings was a deadly cargo of rockets.

The rockets were manufactured in the northern enclave of the Reich, in the rump that was left around the city of Hamburg, but we had succeeded in airlifting them down to Riem. At last we had the weapon with which we could guarantee to shoot down at least one bomber, and today was to be our first attack with an entire formation—three flights of three aircraft each.

When we sighted the first flight of Fortresses it was surrounded by burst clouds from our heavy flak. Countless dwindling puffs of dirty brown smoke made a kind of blizzard of giant snowflakes along the path of the bomber stream.

The bombers were like flocks of birds, their sharp silhouettes visible as far as the eye could see against the intense blue of the sky. Fighters flew with them, and since they were faster they swung to and fro above the formation they were escorting. The size of pinheads, they were visible one moment and invisible the next.

The general clearly wanted to hold the attack until the bombers had flown through the flak belt. We pulled round in a wide turn to get into the best position, and as we did so we saw the bomb carpet unrolling over the terraces, streets, and factories of the outskirts of the city, fountains of earth and bursts of flame marking the swath of destruction.

He ought to go in now, I thought. We must take our chance with the flak; our flying time was limited, and the leading formation of the bombers lay there as if someone had handed it to us on a plate. Its fighter escort we could ignore.

The same thought had evidently occurred to Galland, because with a crisp announcement over the intercom he pulled his aircraft round and went into the attack. Some of the flak was wild and some of it was accurate. One of the giant birds began to cock its right wing and very gradually tipped over, getting farther and farther away from its formation until it was plunging headlong earthward. Several Boeings were towing long white trails from the roots of their wings, and suddenly there was an enormous red flash where the leader of the leading formation had been flying a moment before.

I knew from long experience the effect this kind of spectacle had on bomber pilots' ability to fly in tight formation. They became nervous and fidgety, began to weave up and down, their spacing became irregular—and the whole formation disintegrated. Our second flight was in attacking position and fired its rockets. I followed the long corkscrew trails of the rocket engines with my eyes and actually saw the warheads hit the bombers' metal flanks—followed immediately by two shattering explosions.

The third Me seemed to be having trouble getting rid of his rockets. Instead of following the first two as they let their colossal speed plus pull them high over the bomber formation he appeared to be making a beeline for a Boeing that was flying on its own. In seconds the distance between them shrank to nothing, and the Me scythed off the Boeing's gigantic tail fin with its wing. The metal monstrosity—equipped with more than twenty machine guns and carrying a crew of nine—rolled clumsily onto its back before abruptly going into a vertical dive and disappearing from my view.

I did not see what happened to the Me after the collision, but I mentally wrote off both aircraft and pilot.

I had watched the spectacle with bated breath. Now I concentrated on the task of picking out what would be the best target for my flight without getting in the way of the flight coming in behind me. The smoke trails left by the Fortresses that had been shot down hung eerily in the still air. Pulling gently to starboard I was able to get the remains of a flight of bombers framed in my windshield. They had adopted a policy of every man for himself and were trying to flee westward as fast as they could go.

At that moment my eye fell on a vast cloud of dust and burning fuel that was spreading sluggishly over the eastern edge of the city. Through this murky veil I recognized the hangars, runway, and light-colored perimeter road of our airfield.

They had attacked Riem!

Shortly before this Major Roell had been on his way from Feldkirchen to Riem airfield. As "Kommissar"—a title (borrowed from the Russians) that was coming increasingly into use to express the special powers and responsibilities attached to a particular office—he was in charge of all the airfield's installations and seeing that they functioned properly. He and his driver took shelter from the bombers in the ditch at the side of the road, and for the half-hour that it took until the flak stopped and the last flight of bombers was on its way home he followed the drama being played out in the sky above him, counting the kills and watching the parachutes sink slowly earthward like strings of pearls behind the plunging bombers. He looked toward Riem and all he could see was one enormous cloud enveloping the airfield, the hangars, and the parking areas. All of a sudden it was very quiet; there was only the drone of engines dying away to the west.

Standing up and turning back to his jeep—still undecided whether to drive straight to the airfield, since the sirens had not yet sounded the all-clear—Roell saw a couple of kilometers away the white canopies of several parachutes gliding silently toward the ground. He clearly made out the bodies dangling to and fro beneath them before the trees and roofs obscured his view of the actual landing.

"Come on," he told his driver. "Let's bag them—they're Amis. Our best way is through the grounds of the SS riding school."

This institution was situated in the immediate vicinity of the airfield, and, since it was run by the SS as if these were days of the serenest peace or as if cavalry were some miracle weapon that was being held in reserve, it had long been a thorn in our flesh.

Roell drove down the narrow path that led past the racecourse enclosure and another field laid out as a jumping course. As he shot through the gate leading to the almost endless rows of stables he heard shouting and several shots. Parking the jeep between the rows of stables he hurried toward a group of people crowded round one of the stable doors. As he approached he heard more shots.

The grooms and "stable boys"—they were all female—stood gesticulating nervously outside the dark entrance from which came a blend of shouting, neighing, and snorting.

The doors and windows were all blown in. The shell must have fallen very close, and the ground was littered with tile fragments. Yet despite this impression of chaos Roell was captivated by the sight of the "stable boys." In their tight sweaters and elegant jodhpurs they presented a most curious contrast to their distinctly brutal environment of booted and spurred SS men. A gigantic fellow with scars on his face and wearing riding boots and a blood-spattered white coat was evidently the vet. The SS officer commanding the riding school appeared in the doorway, pistol in hand.

"He's shot the remounts!" shrieked the girls. "Magnificent horses—God, what those animals have been through. . . ."

At this moment a small Opel truck turned in through the gate and drove up between the rows of stables toward them. An infantryman

stood on the platform behind the cab, forage cap pulled down over
his ears to stop it blowing off. As the vehicle pulled up with a jerk the
soldier vaulted over the side and landed on all fours beside the stable
door. Picking himself up and wiping his hands on his thighs, he announced loudly to the bystanders, "We've picked up two Amis—two
airmen. They were shot down and landed by parachute. They're
wounded. . . ."

Immediately the assembled men and girls crowded round the truck
to peer over the sides.

One of the Americans sat with legs outstretched, leaning against
the back of the cab. The other lay curled up in a corner with his face
in his hands. Both seemed to be wounded; their olive flying suits were
mottled with darker patches of blood. The one sitting up was obviously a tall, powerfully built specimen. He was bare-headed; the wind
must have torn his helmet off when he baled out. He had a flat,
coarse-featured face, and his hair was cut short. He returned their
look with a smile, his big blue eyes innocent of fear. It was as if im-
prisonment and all the things that might now happen to him were
nothing compared to the fact that he had been given his life back.
The one lying on the floor was taking no notice of his surroundings.
Moaning quietly, he held his hands pressed to his face. There was
blood on his fingers.

The bystanders were clearly embarrassed and at a loss what to do.
The SS people turned to Roell and whisperingly asked his advice.

"What are we going to do with them? Isn't there an army post or
a POW camp in the area?"

As they stood around undecided, the din from the stables getting
louder again, Roell suddenly heard a babble of voices behind him and
turned to see a group of women come hurrying through the gate and
swarm breathlessly round the parked truck. They were ordinary
housewives dressed in the kind of flowered-print coats that women
wear to do their housework. Their faces were flushed from running,
and some had strands of hair that had come loose and were dangling
down.

Roell shrank back from the cold hatred in their eyes. They fell
silent now as one of their number stepped forward and said, "We
want the swine. We want to finish them off the way they've finished
off our whole street on the estate!" Immediately the babble of voices

rose again, hysterically aggressive, and the women pressed round the truck.

The SS commander was still standing in the stable doorway holding his pistol. There was another sudden silence as all eyes were drawn in fascination to the weapon in his hand.

"What are you waiting for, then?" screeched a voice from the crowd. "Go on—shoot the swine! Goebbels told us what to do with the bastards, didn't he? Kill them!"

The propaganda minister had in fact recently asked the German people the cynical question whether it was not time to have done with all this humanitarian nonsense with regard to "murderers" who brutally killed women and children.

The embarrassed SS officer sought to evade this challenge by backing toward the refuge of the stable door. This appeared to send the women completely out of their minds and they began wildly shouting: "Go on—let them have it! It's all the swine deserve!" Suddenly some of them had fenceposts in their hands; others had picked up stones.

Roell had been watching the scene with growing anxiety. The eyes of the American pilot, now full of fear, were appealing to him for help. Without any hesitation he leapt on to the running-board of the truck and barked at the driver, who was still sitting at the wheel: "Drive off—quickly! Get going!" The engine roared to life and the truck leapt into motion as stones began to clatter on the platform and hit the wings. They reached the main road unharmed and there Roell transferred to his own jeep, which had followed, and ordered the truck driver to stay behind him.

After the first army hospital they stopped at refused to take the prisoners Roell managed to get them admitted to Eglfing-Haar mental hospital—and safety.

The bombers were now in a state of utter confusion. Although for the second time I had been unable to fire my rockets, the other pilots had scored hits. The escort of Mustangs and Lightnings dived down at us and came at us from ahead and out of wild banking turns—all without beginning to constitute a serious hindrance to us.

Our tiny formation had "split at the seams," and we each moved independently through the milling turmoil of bombers and fighters, exploiting our far superior speed. The scale of circling, climbing, and diving maneuvers was so vast with the Me 262 that at times they carried us far away from the action and made the bombers and escort fighters appear to hang motionless in the air.

I decided not to fly a second attack because I wanted to get back to the airfield with sufficient fuel in reserve. The American fighters would undoubtedly take advantage of our vulnerability during landing and keep an eye on the airfield with the object of shooting us down as we came in.

I circled Riem at high speed to give myself an idea of the situation. Though pock-marked by the explosion of innumerable small shells, the actual airfield appeared to have received only a fraction of the bombers' cargo of destruction. The adjacent estate toward the riding school and the racecourse had come off worse. I saw an Me come in over the perimeter road and land on a strip of grass between craters. Seconds later I was on the ground myself and the mechanics were waving me over to a splinter box in a distant corner of the field, leading the way with the jeep.

Six of the Flying Fortresses had come down in flames; two others had embarked on the homeward run severely damaged. We had shown convincingly that a concentric operation with jet fighters would put a stop to the bomb terror. Galland's theory that hitting the enemy with a mere eighty Me 262s would stop the daylight raids clearly held water. The Americans after all had interrupted their air offensive for weeks following their experience at Schweinfurt in October 1943. The loss of sixty-five aircraft, each carrying a crew of ten— making 650 men who had taken years to train—prompted Congress to discuss whether it was possible to go on flying such raids at all.

All our aircraft returned from the mission with the exception of Unteroffizier Schallmoser's. He was the one who, lacking aerial-combat experience, had rammed a Boeing. He subsequently baled out and landed safely by parachute.

Fighter Unit 44 (also known as the Galland Unit) constituted a rather special undertaking. After being dismissed in disgrace from his post as General of Fighter Pilots, Galland was given permission to organize a fighter squadron of his own. In it all the senior Jagdwaffe officers on longer commanding units—highly decorated fighter pilots to a man—were given an opportunity to do their bit against the enemy air forces.

Prominent among them was the group of former commanders who in January 1945 had sought from Generaloberst von Greim and General Koller permission personally to inform the Supreme Commander of the Wehrmacht (Hitler!) [author's parentheses] of the bitterness of their troops at Göring's unfair charges that they lacked fighting spirit and to present to him proposals regarding a more appropriate use of the Jagdwaffe. The attempt, however, had ended with Göring himself receiving a delegation of fighter commanders led by Oberst Lützow, listening to what they had to say, and terminating the discussion by calling their action "mutiny" and threatening to have Oberst Lützow shot. . . .

Galland organized the unit in Brandenburg before moving it down to Munich-Riem and leading it in a series of highly successful missions.

"History of Aerial Warfare" Study Group
Major General Grabmann (retired)
Historical Division of the U.S. Army

10
Munich-Riem
18 April 1945

In the early part of April the Allies, enjoying undisputed air supremacy over the Reich, stepped up their air offensive to unprecedented
proportions. The war had entered its final phase.

Lightnings and Mustangs had our airfield under observation as
soon as the weather was fit for flying. We were spending as much time
on standby as we had at the beginning of the war. Our little unit was
the Luftwaffe. The scrap of geography that we were defending was
tiny and getting smaller every day. Yet as if by a miracle we had
enough ammunition, enough spares—and more aircraft than we
could use.

Early in the morning of 18 April 1945 I drove to our operations
room in Feldkirchen. The red disk of the sun had just crept over the
horizon and was attempting to disperse the white veils of mist that
lay over the fields and meadows around the village. In an hour at
most the fighters would be there. After that the first reports of the
bombers setting out from Italy and England would start coming in
from our radio monitoring service. And around noon we would be
taking off—as we did every day.

We had developed our combat reconnaissance to a degree of perfection that was out of all proportion to the handful of aircraft we

were able to put in the air. The radio monitoring service gave warning of an intrusion as soon as the bombers synchronized frequencies after the start and began talking to one another. They had now abandoned the exemplary radio discipline that they had maintained until quite recently (what was the point, they probably thought, since the Luftwaffe was dead?) and held spirited conversations from aircraft to aircraft as if they had been standing at the bar. As soon as the radar installations of our "island" had sighted the enemy they reported location and height and the number of bombers to be expected. The entire aircraft warning service of the southern Bavarian enclave was working for us.

The large schoolhouse lay at the edge of the village; looking west on a clear day one could see Riem airfield. One wall of the classroom bore a huge blackboard with a box for sponge and chalks. The sit. map on the long, windowless wall, an enormous panel of frosted glass, was divided into squares that were identified with large red letters. The cities of Munich, Augsburg, Regensburg, and Nuremberg appeared as red patches the size of fists.

The white-coated assistants burst into their usual flurry of activity as Lützow and I came in. They were better-looking than the usual run of *Blitz* girls. The tall, pigtailed one with the powerful legs would thrust out her breasts aggressively against the starched coat as soon as one came near her. The thin blonde in the high heels was waxen-faced with lack of sleep. Her soulful eyes threw me a reproachful look before she began ostentatiously working on the sit. map, her slender, shapely calves showing to advantage as she stood on tiptoe to crayon in the bombers' course.

The previous evening's discussion—I mostly talked with Lützow, sometimes with the general—had been characterized by the usual ghastly futility. We were fleeing from ourselves as well as from reality. Another five days, a week, perhaps a fortnight? And then? The nearer the inevitable approached the more we avoided talking about it. And we felt steadily more ashamed, seeing the end coming but no longer finding the courage to speak the truth.

Although numerous Reich potentates had withdrawn to the Alpine Fortress and we were nominally subordinate to a flying corps, virtually no one took any notice of our existence anymore. They were all much too busy preparing their exits, and in any case they could take no further pleasure in playing with the Luftwaffe's last operational unit. Göring had left Berlin and was on his way to Obersalzberg via Bohemia, accompanied by the Chief of the Luftwaffe General Staff. But he had lost all interest in the "mutineers'" squadron.

The light flak opened up outside the windows. Patches of mist still obscured visibility but one could hear the drone of Lightnings' engines and the howl as they nose-dived.

"Splendid," muttered Lützow ironically. "They're after a few more quick kills. Taking off and landing we're sitting ducks. But from tomorrow on Sachsenberg is going to fly cover for us with his Focke-Wulf fighters."

Leutnant Sachsenberg, son of the First World War "*Pour le Mérite*" hero, had announced his eagerness to provide fighter cover for us with the new Focke-Wulf. "You can keep your jets," he had said. "I'm no speed merchant. I prefer to hung Lightnings the old-fashioned way."

We went out of the building and down the steps to join the general in his jeep for the drive to the airfield. "Approaching from both directions as usual," I said. "Takeoff around 11.00 hours."

"Look at that for a piece of criminal stupidity!" exclaimed the general suddenly as we turned through the gate in the barbed-wire fence onto the grass of the airfield. A light flak battery was taking up position just inside the fence; circular banks of earth had been thrown up as emplacements for 20mm guns. "Hell, Macky—they're only girls! Pull up a minute."

And girls they were. They had even made some elegant tailoring adjustments to their blue-grey uniforms so that the trousers sat tightly over the behind and their tunics were neatly "waisted." They were leaping busily about, not without a certain pride in their bearing: they were "on duty."

"What's going on here?" asked the general, looking down into one of the pits in which a double-barreled flak gun was just being mounted.

Out of the seething blue-grey mass of doggedly determined female soldiery a lone male figure—that of a bombardier of astonishingly impressive build—shot stiffly to attention.

"*Herr General*," he stammered with an effort, "we are preparing a position."

"I can see that," the general snarled. "But don't you fellows realize that . . ." At this point, however, he appeared to realize himself that the bombardier was not the proper target for his criticism. "Where's your battery commander?" he asked sharply.

"*Herr Oberleutnant, Herr Oberleutnant!*" the bombardier shouted across to the next emplacement. Meanwhile his female crew had thrown itself amateurishly to attention. The lieutenant came dashing over. A man of about fifty, he was tall and skinny and wore thick-lensed spectacles that gave his sunken eyes an even more school-masterly look. Raising a slender, manicured hand in the "German salute," he planted himself before the general and stood there motion-less.

"For God's sake, man!" said the general. "What do you think you're doing, putting a light battery in here? And with girls, if you please!"

"*Herr General . . .*"

"'*Herr General*' be blowed—at ease and tell me what you think you're up to."

The girls were watching the three officers closely, almost devouring the general with their eyes. And that day the general really was the battle-tried hero incarnate. The grey leather flying-suit with the fur collar and the legs with their bulging pockets pulled down over his fur boots made him look almost like something from Mars. The quite improbably misshapen officer's cap (as if he went under the shower with it) was pulled down low over his eyes so that the peak touched the enormous oval frames of the sunglasses perched precariously on his broad, battered nose. The moustache and the black Brazil hanging out of the corner of his mouth completed the martial portrait.

"Sir, I have orders to install my light battery here at the edge of the field and protect the jets during takeoff against enemy fighters." It was said with more than a hint of pride.

"Have you at least got slit trenches?"

"We are digging trenches now, sir."

"Well, for God's sake get on with it right away," said the general urgently. "Take a lesson from what the Fortresses did yesterday with their little fragmentation bombs. Get them dug and get them covered up! When they hit us next time it won't be funny, I'm telling you."

"*Jawohl, Herr General.*"

The nice schoolteacher gave us another salute and the girls, who had begun whispering among themselves, turned back to their work.

"Downright criminal negligence—it's an outrage! Imagine the bloodbath when the *Viermots* drop their load. Those poor girls . . ."

We drove round the perimeter road, noting that our unit had meanwhile grown into a respectable fighting force. The ground crews, working nonstop, had repaired, refueled, and reloaded the aircraft and dispersed them around the field with the aid of special track-laying motorcycles.

The squadron's rest area was a masterpiece of improvisation, consisting basically of a table and a few rickety chairs set up in the middle of a patch of weeds and undergrowth. A field telephone stood on the table. The pilots lounged in deck chairs sipping coffee out of chunky Wehrmacht cups. Saucers of thin red jam and a stack of slices of damp army bread covered some of the cup rings on the stained tabletop and provided our sustenance. The morning was very chilly, with several strata of light cloud obscuring our view of the Alps.

For the thousandth time we sat down to endure the agony of waiting before a scramble. No one felt like talking, so we sat in silence. The road that ran past outside the airport fence was deserted. Looking west, one could see the greyish silhouette of the roofs and churches of Munich—an unreal, shadowy mass, as if the city was dead and abandoned.

They were all looking pretty seedy and pale, I thought. We were like dayflies who had come to the end of their day, where the dream dissolves into nothingness. Why did we still fly? Whom were we doing it for? I had no idea, for example, what the general thought when he was not flying, or when he sat in his chair in the ops room, staring straight ahead of him with a cigar in the corner of his mouth. A lot of drinking went on every evening. Fährmann had been looking even paler than usual since his bale-out. He was another one with an impossible cap—all jaunty creases. He wore it all the time except in bed. He had a narrow, finely chiseled face, and from the corners of his mouth two knife-sharp folds fell all the way to his chin.

He replaced the receiver on the field telephone. "They've just flown over Stuttgart. Pretty slow—must be a biggish formation."

"We don't want to take off too early," said the general. "Macky, you lead the second flight. . . ."

"Right," I said.

There was no wind. It would be a long ground run before the aircraft lifted off. My machine was armed with twenty-four rockets under the wings and the cannon had full magazines—an enormous weight for so light an aircraft.

"Get me operational HQ." I heard Galland's voice repeating "Mainz—heading for Darmstadt" and "lots, with fighter escort," and my imagination began to work. We would be meeting them somewhere between Stuttgart and Munich. I would let Galland lead his flight into the attack before I followed up. We must try and stay in safety as long as we could. Our work would be easiest if Galland managed to break up the formation.

It was not fear that suddenly welled up in me but simply the cold realization that I was once more about to expose myself to the risk of flying straight into the concentrated defensive fire of hundreds of machine guns. Even if my chance of destroying one or more bombers were enormously increased with this high-speed aircraft and its deadly arsenal of weapons, an attack was still an attack. How did one bale out of a jet fighter at 8,000 meters? Would the parachute open? And if it did wouldn't it be torn to shreds immediately? Or freeze solid, because at that altitude temperatures were an inhuman −40–50°C? Would it not be better to free-fall to an altitude where the temperature was more tolerable? But how did one do that? It was something I had never tried.

"In about ten minutes," Galland announced.

Fährmann put his cupped hands to his mouth and shouted across to the mechanics: "Takeoff in ten minutes! Two flights—the general and Oberst Steinhoff leading."

The men, who were busy digging slit trenches, downed tools and ran over to their respective charges. They still obeyed every order with stolid willingness.

"You must hold the brakes on until the turbines are revving full," I repeated mentally to myself. "If you let her run right to the edge of the airfield and only pull the stick then, you'll have more speed and you'll lift off more easily." But it was a dangerous maneuver. If the flaps failed to work the aircraft would not take off—and that would be that. "I wonder if they'll attack Munich—or Regensburg or Nuremberg? Or our airfield? We mustn't leave it too late. It'll be lawful if they start laying a bomb carpet just as we're taking off. . . ."

"Keep close beside me, count," I said aloud to Krupinski. "As soon as I've fired my rockets you go into the attack."

This was obvious, of course, then Krupinski simply said, "Right," accepting the unnecessary order for what it was: an attempt to kill the remaining minutes before takeoff. Fährmann shot me a sidelong glance and started pulling on his gloves ("Can't be long now."). Hein Wübke rubbed the back of a hand across his mouth and said, "I know why you're not taking me—the trains aren't running anymore." This raised a welcome laugh all round. Wübke had had "I fly for the Reichsbahn" painted in large white letters on the fuselage of his Me. Asked what the inscription meant, he replied, "Well, I always come back by train." He had in fact returned from his last three missions by rail. He had been shot down and baled out a total of four times in succession. "Pick out the best kite you can find," the general had told him, indicating the reserve aircraft on the parking area. "We've got any number of them. Word seems to have gotten around that we're collecting stray Mes. Soon we won't know what to do with them."

"They're heading for Regensburg—lots of bombers. If you take off now we'll be just right," Fährmann announced as he replaced the receiver again.

"Let's go," said the general, stubbing out his cigar in ꞏꞏucer and clambering to his feet.

The sirens began to wail as we hurried across to the aircraft. My Me 262 was parked immediately in front of the high wall that bordered the airfield to the west. I ran quickly round her once before getting in. I ducked under the wing and felt the rockets with my hand; I pulled the slotted flap out of the leading edge, letting it spring back with a loud clack. As I placed my foot in the recess and heaved myself up over the side of the cockpit, I ran my other hand over the smooth fuselage—the way one strokes a horse's neck. She was a very good aircraft and I had been flying her ever since we had started forming the unit in Brandenburg. Of course she too had her little ailments from time to time and had to be left with the ground crew while I flew a spare machine. But somehow she just suited me. I did not need to trim her when she was hurtling along at maximum speed; I could take my hands off the stick and let her fly herself. I have known men refuse to go up when "their" machine was not clear for takeoff. After a mission the pilots would discuss the aircraft as if they had been racehorses: "Ah, you were in Yellow Seven, no wonder you had problems. She's no good—too slow . . ." Or: "Number Four, now—there's a kite for you."

Once in the cockpit I wriggled around on the parachute until I found the right position, hitching myself up with both hands on the cockpit rim. It always took me about a minute to get comfortable. The seat was adjustable to bring one's eyes exactly on a level with the sight. I slipped on my shoulder belts and waist belt and pulled them nice and tight, then buckled my helmet under my chin. I picked up the oxygen mask ("The lips of the indicator must move open and shut when the oxygen is flowing.") Meanwhile my eyes had flashed over the instruments. I set the altimeter for barometric pressure, moved the ailerons with my feet, checked the rudder with the control stick, and switched on the radio. I was ready.

I saw the general stick his right hand out of the cockpit and wave it in a circle. A mechanic started the little motors at the front of the turbines, and the turbines fired and began to hum. Temperature normal, air pressure normal, close cockpit, taxi into position.

I had only to turn the aircraft into the wind and the flag-lined runway stretched away before me. The general's flight moved off with turbines screaming, their exhaust rocking my Me quite violently. The penetrating smell of kerosene filled the cockpit.

When the three shapes had disappeared in a towering cloud of dust and fumes, I eased the throttle forward and took my toes off the brake pedals. With a gentle shudder the aircraft began to move.

Suddenly I was humming to myself: the tension had fallen away from one second to the next. Out of the corners of my eyes I saw the other two following me to port and starboard. The aircraft bumped clumsily over the grass, its undercarriage making muffled noises as the heavy weight bounced up and down. How ungainly the thing was on the ground!

And then that curious feeling of power and superiority swept over me, as it did every time I took off in the Me 262. The question why I flew, why I was a fighter pilot, simply receded into the background. The Americans had reached Crailsheim, the Russians were advancing on Berlin, and the Luftwaffe—apart from us—no longer existed. It was a dangerous kind of therapy I was using! Worse—it was an insane piece of self-deception.

She's too heavy, I thought half unconsciously. The field was extremely bumpy and uneven; the previous day's bomb carpet had made innumerable shallow craters that had been filled in in a somewhat makeshift fashion.

I saw the general lift out of the dust cloud in front of me and retract his undercarriage. At that moment the silhouette of his Me began to wander to starboard: my machine was changing direction although, having reacted automatically, I was already countering with the rudder.

In five years of war I had seen danger approaching in a wide variety of guises. My reaction too had varied from the sneaking fear before a hopelessly risky mission to the outright panic that takes your breath away and paralyses your nervous system. When Spitfires had chased me over the rooftops of Rotterdam or when Lightnings, having shot my aircraft up over the Balkans, had moved in for the kill, my determination not to die had found expression in prompt action. When, reduced to passively registering the fact that my possibilities of action were exhausted, I had landed in the Stalingrad pocket with no undercarriage and my engine belching smoke, or when Russian infantry had riddled my Me 109 with a hail of bullets as I flew low over the lines, making me sink like a sick bird into the snowdrifts along the Don—every time my mind, reacting with machinelike precision, had come up smartly with that swift calculation of the chances for survival by which hope is fed. In the few seconds following the moment in which I realized that the aircraft was going into a skid and saw out of the corner of my eye the great tongue of flame that had turned one turbine into a gigantic blowtorch—this time my mind signaled finality! My brain, knowing no answer, capitulated. "This is it," I heard myself say. "It's happening. You can't stop now, you're already much too fast." The embankment along which the perimeter road ran was only two hundred meters ahead. "Pull the stick back hard!"—but she was too heavy and refused to fly.

When the undercarriage hit the embankment the Me reared up as if caught by one of those hard gusts of wind that you get on a hot summer's day. The shock was not cruel and final, not the death smash of an elegant and extremely vulnerable masterpiece of technology against a solid obstacle. Instead it was as if the aircraft were making a desperate attempt to lift off into its element in spite of everything—although the last, muffled blow had ushered in its final destruction: crashdown, fire, explosion!

Catapulted high into the air, the stricken bird dragged itself through several more seconds of existence. Shortly before the impact my hands flew instinctively to the shoulder belts. I tugged so violently on the straps that my body slammed back against the seat. Then, all of a sudden, everything seemed to grow still. There was only the hissing of the huge flames. As if in slow motion I saw a wheel go soaring through the air. Metal fragments and bits of undercarriage flew after it, spinning very slowly. Wherever I looked was red, deep red.

I saw in that moment, right before my eyes, the grey, totally disfigured face of the man who had been burned.

It was 1943. I had combined a brief spell of front leave with a trip to Bavaria to celebrate Barkhorn's wedding. It was hardly a time for celebrating and making merry, but we enjoyed to the full those few days' lease of life.

The air was cold and crisp as my wife and I alighted from the train at Tegernsee. Beneath the broad overhang of the station roof one could see the peaks of the Alps. Walking down the platform toward the exit, I took my wife's arm and started chatting easily and gaily about the prospect of spending a few days with friends in this almost peaceful corner of our country.

We came out of the station into bright daylight—and suddenly there was this man in front of me. He was extremely thin and wore the elegant waisted coat of an army officer. Beneath the peak of the officer's cap the face had been burned away. We almost collided. He had his arm in that of a young woman, who was leading him; clearly he was blind. There was so little room and the encounter had happened so suddenly that I found myself executing several of those clumsy dodging movements that do nothing to resolve such embarrassing situations before my wife managed to pull me to one side.

The sight of that utterly ruined face filled me with horror. In fact it was a face no longer; where the face had been was now a grey, spongy flatness. Only the pouting, blood-red lips stood up out of what was just a ghastly, revolting mess. An enormous pair of dark glasses did something to mitigate the hideousness of the apparition. The woman holding his arm was young and very beautiful. She held the arm tightly to her side and was talking to the man incessantly; I do not think she had even noticed our presence.

During the battle for England and later during the fighting over Sicily and the "Reich Defense" missions against the four-engined bombers I had spent many a night expelling from my mind the innumerable variations on the theme of injury and death that filled the limbo between sleep and waking with their phantoms. But ever since my meeting with the "faceless man" the fear had been growing in me that my aircraft might one day catch fire and I might suffer the same fate.

I now saw that ruined face before me as if projected on a red wall of flame, and it seemed to me I sat for a long time in the wreckage of my cockpit, staring at the vision. Again my mind registered: "It's happened." Then my hands began to work with feverish urgency, yet as fast and as accurately as if they had been pieces of machinery: "Release waist belt, grasp parachute catch with right hand, turn clockwise, and punch." Off came the canopy and I was staring out at the field, at the turbine that had been torn off the wing and was bouncing over the soft ground, and at the puddles of fuel spreading over the green grass and bursting into fresh sheets of towering orange flame. Two, three breaths and I was inhaling fire. It felt as if a pair of iron tongs had been clamped round my chest.

"You've got to get out of here," my mind told me, and to egg myself on I started shouting "Out, out!" over and over again. Grasping the sides of the cockpit, I pulled myself up until I was standing on the parachute ("Out, out!"). I had got my feet over the cockpit rim when the rockets started exploding under the wings. They skittered wildly over the field and went off with a hellish bang. Taking great leaping strides I ran out along the wing to escape from the flames. And when I emerged from the inferno and my straining lungs filled with fresh air I sank to my knees as if under the impact of a mighty blow.

"Get up and go farther. Quick—get up and go farther." I managed to get to my feet, and as I stumbled a few steps farther everything went black: my eyes had swollen shut. I became aware of piercing pain in my wrists where the flames shooting up through the cockpit floor had burned off the skin between my gloves and the sleeves of my leather jacket.

As I caught my foot in a furrow and pitched headlong I heard a man's voice say:

"Here, I'll give you a hand. My car's just over there. Put your arm round my shoulder and we'll get you to hospital."

*   *   *

The insidious dreamworld in which I was to spend many weeks was ushered in by the prick of a needle containing a powerful painkilling opiate. From then on I experienced my surroundings only acoustically, through the colorful veil of imagination. My eyes were closed and my whole face covered with thick white gauze. Noises reached my ears muffled, as if from a great distance, suddenly to become alarmingly loud. The silent, drugged nights I spent gliding through thick jungle, and when the shock I had undergone rose to the surface of consciousness, panic cramped my chest.

They wheeled me on a hard trolley down dully echoing corridors to the operating theater. The doctor touched me with his hands and talked to me, but only scraps of what he was saying reached me. They washed their hands, the water running endlessly. I heard the sound of scrubbing as they made trivial conversation and laughed together. Why don't they get on with it? I could not articulate. "All right, all right," said the doctor. Suddenly it was very quiet. I felt no pain; in fact I felt almost happy in a delicious state of weightless floating. "Keep still now, quite still," said the nurse. I supposed I was back in my bed. Perhaps it was not so bad after all, perhaps just a few scars?

The days, the start of which I recognized by the sounds of the hospital waking up or because the nurse came to take my temperature and try to introduce the straw for the liquid food between my lips, were endless. People fussed round me all the time, but I just wanted to sleep. They injected opiates, "Dolantin," pain-killing drugs ("As long as his strength keeps up!"). The front seemed to be close; they carted me along corridors to the air-raid shelter and back up to my room at more and more frequent intervals.

Galland came to see me and spoke of the squadron. It could not go on much longer, he thought, with the Americans before Augsburg and the Allies in possession of the Po Valley and advancing toward the Brenner Pass. I registered it all as if he had been speaking to me through a thick wall, and since I was not capable of reacting in any way he gave up. He seemed to stay sitting by my bed for a while, then he touched me and whispered, "See you, Macky." I heard the door shut and realized he had left the room.

Then suddenly Rieber, my fat batman, was sitting beside the bed. It had been a day of excruciating agony. They had wheeled me along the corridor again: operating theater, air-raid shelter, dressing—with overwhelming pain ("He's getting weaker and more sensitive all the time")—and begging for a painkiller. Under the bandages a nauseating putrescence had set in, with the skin breaking up into innumerable pus corpuscles. It was as if ants were swarming over my whole face.

I was aware of the increasing nervousness of those around me. They were obviously scared. When the bombs fell they were silent, but afterward they began feverishly whispering together.

"We're moving you, sir," said Rieber. "You can't stay here. The Amis will be in Munich soon, and anyway the staff here are all cracking up."

I tried to convey that I thought this was a good idea by carefully nodding my head.

"We're taking you up to Bad Wiessee, on the Tegernsee. There's a smashing hospital there."

They took me up to Bad Wiessee in an ambulance one night and there gave me injections to make me sleep till late morning. Then the new doctor arrived with his train of attendants: "Don't worry, sir—we'll patch this up all right." His voice sounded nice. The new nurses introduced themselves, including Nurse Maria who took me particularly in charge, cared for me for weeks, and looked, when in May the bandages were first removed from my eyes, completely different from the way I had imagined her.

Suddenly Rieber was back beside my bed: "I'll be staying with you now. Who do you think's going to feed you?" And: "I've organized masses of eggs to get you on your feet again." There he sat patiently beside my bed, feeding me, driving away the flies, and describing to me the things I could not see.

"The hospital is in an old villa not far from the lake. The doctors are excellent and the food's good too." But knowing how weak I was he soon fell silent, though he did not abandon his post by my bed.

Once, waking out of a shallow sleep and a series of crazy dreams, I heard Galland's voice: "Macky, can you hear me?" he asked quietly.

It was several minutes before I knew where I was, and my heart began thumping as everything I had been stemming off in my drugged twilight state came washing over me: the airfield and the smell of kerosene and the takeoff and the flames. . . .

"You needn't answer. Just raise your hand if you understand me."

"I can understand you all right, sir," I said. "I may say some funny things but they stick so many needles into me . . . You'll have to forgive me."

"Macky, I was admitted here yesterday. I stopped a bit of shrapnel attacking *Viermots*. In the knee—it's not too bad."

I gave my sign of life and nodded.

"I hear you're doing well—mending nicely. Don't worry about a thing."

Another long pause. I wanted to ask about the others, about how much longer the war would go on and whether they had had any losses. I heard him clear his throat.

"Listen, Macky—Lützow didn't get back from a mission against the *Viermots* over the Swabian Jura. I'm sorry. . . ."

My heart leapt into my throat as a wave of uncontrollable emotion took hold of me. With appalling clarity I grasped the full significance of the news. A period of the most intense companionship with a friend was over, and the pain hit me as something that was exclusively mine. Our discussions about questions of loyalty and the madness of the way the war was being conducted had been concentrated and occasionally passionate. But we had always found our way to a measure of agreement that had given me the equanimity I needed to get through the last months of the catastrophe. We had become close during the difficult days of the defense of Sicily. Of similar temperament, both of us critical and often too quick to speak our minds, we had racked ourselves with doubts and still found no alternative to flying, fighting, and shooting. We had taken to conspiracy when it was already much too late—and we knew it.

He had played his part as spokesman of the little group of insurgent officers with courage and had clearly derived satisfaction from doing so. I should never forget how he had stood up in front of Göring and thundered, "If you interrupt me, *Herr Reichsmarschall*, if you stop me before I have said all I have to say, this whole discussion is pointless." But he had come back to us from his exile merely pessimistic. He could not even enjoy flying the new jet fighter. All he saw was the end, only a matter of days away, and he was gloomy and despondent.

I do not recollect what else Galland said; I was too wrapped up in myself and in the thought of my dead friend. Possibly nothing else was said at all, for Galland knew what Lützow had meant to me.

Then he left, and in the silence that settled round me I was seized by an overwhelming feeling of depression. I was reduced to gasping for breath and trying vainly to sit up in bed.

I sank back on the pillows exhausted just as the nurse came in to feed me. Rolling onto my side, I motioned to her to give me my sleeping jab. I did not feel like eating; I just wanted to be left alone. It was all over now, this was the end, my world lay in ruins. Franzl Lützow was dead!

And I remembered how as young Luftwaffe lieutenants we had sung, "*We shall march on though ruins surround us. . . .*"

Epilogue

Oberföhring Army Hospital, Munich
September 1945

One day here is very much like another. The summer has been hot, and now, with the leaves beginning to turn, Indian summer is in the air. As if nature were determined to show that she can still prevail over so much stupidity, destructiveness, and cruelty, the rose borders and beds of autumn flowers in front of the barracks are a riot of color.

The monotony of hospital life is beginning to get on our nerves. The old familiar doctors were demobbed long ago; the new ones look in occasionally to say a few noncommittal words but otherwise leave us and our problems alone. There are only "serious cases" left here. We "facial burns" are among them, and we get the feeling that people have not quite made up their minds what to do with us. The clinics for plastic surgery are not operating yet, and in any case no one appears to have very much experience in this field.

We cling to the daily routine as if it were a military duty roster. After breakfast, as soon as the beds have been made—here Holzamer and I are dependent on others' help as our hands are still thickly bandaged—I start dictating. Holzamer has developed considerable skill at typing with his crippled hands. He sits hunched over the big Remington and, sucking the saliva from the corners of his mouth at regular intervals, he asks me question after question.

The weather prophet can barely restrain his desire to break out and be free. ("I've got to get across before winter sets in. I know the way through the Thuringian Forest like the back of my hand.") As we climb the hill in the evening to look at the sunset (between our legs, of course, bent double) he speaks warmly of his home in Thuringia, its forests and its people, and of his mother.

The hospital has long ceased to be cut off from the outside world. We not only have the radio but we also read the newspapers. They are printed on cheap, unsized paper, but they give us a picture of the extent of the catastrophe, of the concentration camp atrocities, and of the preparations for the Nuremberg Tribunal.

When we came here months ago the world beyond the fence appeared lifeless. Now the bustle seems to increase daily. They are going to work again, on bicycles or walking to the nearby tram stop. There are also more and more cars—no new ones, of course; many of them are veterans, still showing traces of camouflage paint, and there are cast-off jeeps, wood-gas burners, and others that had been "conscripted."

Barter over the fence flourishes. Cigarettes, eggs, even medicine, bandages, scissors, and alcohol (not denatured!) are the new currency. I find the temptation to convert my watch or even my Leica (assuming this has not been "frisked" into new, American ownership) into solid food increasing in proportion as the hospital diet becomes less and less nourishing.

In July I had another trip up to Beuerberg Convent. The University Opthalmic Clinic is housed there because their bombed building in Munich is not yet ready for reoccupation. They wanted to try an eyelid transplant. I have been having a great deal of pain; the corneas threaten to dry out because the lids are so burned they no longer cover my eyes. At any rate Dr. Stumpf, who is touchingly concerned about my case, thought we ought to try.

It was my second visit to Beuerberg; the first had been some two months earlier, when I still lacked the strength to walk.

We were shipped in a convoy of heavy American trucks from Bad Wiessee, where our hospital had been closed down. The GIs drove us through the lovely Upper Bavarian landscape at breakneck speed. At Beuerberg they simply pulled up in front of the convent and dumped their entire cargo of human misery—amputees, blind, bullet wounds, and burns—on the eye clinic, leaving it up to them to sort us out.

They were marvelously restful days. An atmosphere of peace and silence enveloped us immediately in the cells of the convent. The nuns, who provided some of the clinic's nursing staff, outdid one another in deeds of loving kindness, and the nourishing convent food was undoubtedly many calories over the loser's appointed quota.

One day they stood me up and walked me out into the interior courtyard, which was surrounded by a magnificent old cloister. They sat me down on a bench with a number of privates in hideous hospital-issue clothes who were already enjoying the warm May sun. The privates greeted me as an equal, using the familiar *Du* of brothers in affliction. "Hello there," they said, and: "There you are, see? You can do it. Another few days and you'll be hopping round like a weasel."

Pansies and primulas flowered in the beds in the middle of the little courtyard. It was very still, only the nuns in their huge white starched hoods moving soundlessly along the arcades. We all took a typical private's enjoyment in it, almost as if we suspected that the idyll was to be short-lived. Suddenly each of us had a glass of cold, frothy beer in front of him.

"Cigar?" asked my neighbor to the left, giving me a pleasant start. He lit it for me, and with my bandaged hands I carefully raised the precious thing to my lips.

Their conversation gradually faded in my ears until it sounded like something happening a long way off. A feeling of sheer joy at being alive took such immediate possession of me that I had to make an effort to nod polite agreement when addressed. I breathed in the delicious spring air. I was surrounded by men who, like myself, had fought and suffered. They talked of their plans, their homes, their families, wives, children, and girlfriends, and the war seemed as remote as a ghastly dream.

Our peace was rudely disturbed. Suddenly all those hoods were fluttering along the corridors like frightened birds while all around us soldiers vigorously gave vent to their feelings: "No—it can't be true. We want to stay here, we want to stay here!"

"Everyone go to your rooms and pack your things. We're moving out immediately," a medical officer was shouting. Then I saw the GIs. With cries of "Come on, boys—*los, los, snell, snell!*" they tried to hurry us along. When they took my arms to help me to my room I rebelled. "No!" I screamed. "I won't come with you! I've had enough—I can't take any more!"

"Come on," said my companions. "Don't make a fuss, man. They'll take you anyway."

I resisted like a stubborn child, but they carried me bodily along the corridor and put me on my bed while a nun collected my things together.

The convoy of trucks was drawn up on the dusty road in front of the convent. They were open trucks, and the prospect of driving along farm tracks on one of them made me feel physically sick. So I kept up my protest from the bed, repeating monotonously, "They'll not get me out of here, they'll not get me out of here!" But they did. Two of them dumped me unceremoniously on a stretcher, carried me down the stairs, and loaded me—carefully—on the back of a truck. The nun had trotted along beside me, urging me to keep calm. But when she saw the open lorries it took her breath away too. Looking round for someone in authority, she said pleadingly, "You can't do it—his whole face is an open wound!" But a sergeant, obviously the transport commander, stepped up and pushed her aside, shouting, "*Snell, snell*—we're in a hurry."

Just as they were about to close up the tailboard the nun darted forward, tore the enormous butterfly hood from her head, and placed it over my face. I caught a glimpse of cropped hair as she bent over me and said, "To stop the dust." Before I grasped what had happened the tailboard had slammed shut and the truck was rolling off downhill. After a journey of several agonizing hours we were unloaded at Allgasing.

They were not able to operate on my eyelids this time. It was too early, apparently; the scar tissue is still "working," and my face has not yet "settled down." So after a couple of days at Beuerberg I came back to Oberföhring to find that my roommates had been longing for my return. "We missed you," they said.

As we sat around the table that evening I realized for the first time that though we are all in a hurry to get out, at the same time we are afraid of the world beyond the fence. We talk more and more about our relations, not knowing whether they are still alive or not. Since the Russians marched into Thuringia I have been one ambition the poorer; I had hoped to be able to return home. And since the Russians are also in Pomerania and Mecklenburg my thoughts revolve more and more frequently around what had happened to Ursula and the children. Did they manage to get away from the estate in Western Pomerania before the Russian army swept over them?

The thing we had always put off talking about we now discuss every evening: what will we do when we are released? The weather prophet, a doctor of physics *summa cum laude*, already sees himself teaching—at a university, if possible. Holzamer's dream is a job at the Ministry of Finance. ("There'll always be a Ministry of Finance, and I've got my clerk's diploma.") For the count and myself things look less rosy. He is a school-leaver without a trade and I am a philology student without a degree. What are we to do? And there are still these rumors about deporting senior officers.

With the weather prophet busy with his preparations for departure, help has arrived for me from the other side of the fence. It arrived in the form of two ladies in summery dirndl dresses bringing us bulging handbags full of fruit, bread, sausage—and above all books.

Frau von Coester is the mother of the adjutant I lost on the Russian Front. Having heard I was in the hospital here, she came with her friend to get me out. Their helpfulness is overwhelming, their optimism infectious. I'm to apply for my release as quickly as possible. I'm to stay at their place ("But of course!") and start the search for my wife from there. At the same time I can help them get their bookshop started.

Next morning: Removed the bandage from my eyes to find the weather prophet ready to march. He was just securing his iron rations on top of his knapsack. ("I have to get through the forests. It may take me days.") Noticing that I was awake, he said, "I'm off today but I'll be in touch—don't you worry."

Holzamer watched his departure with envy and has hardly said a thing all day, sitting brooding, fiddling with a map of Germany, and occasionally exchanging whispers with the count.

I am to be released tomorrow.

As I turn in the doorway and say, "Look after yourselves," they look at me as if I were a traitor.

Release is a mere formality in my case. My condition, including my inability to hold a pen in my right hand for the vital signature, clearly makes an impression on the American officer. "Good luck," he says, and next minute I am out in the corridor again—"discharged."

Later, waiting at the tram stop with my bulging pilot's knapsack at my feet, I find I am one among many. I am jostled about when the tram arrives and people get out. No one takes any notice of me or helps me get in. The tram is crowded. I stand between the rows of seats with the knapsack between my knees as we clatter through the ravaged city toward the station. I see people in the streets going about their business. They are dressed simply, but the women in their gaily colored summer dresses enliven the desolate spectacle of Munich's ruins. I ride through the streets that have been cleared of rubble and that already offer shops with modest window displays and flowers.

Walking along the platform toward the exit I experience a wave of energy and exhilaration. I am thirty-two years old, one of millions who share the same fate, and I mean to seize my chance!

INDEX OF NAMES

ABOUT THE AUTHOR

Johannes Steinhoff was a colonel in the Luftwaffe during World War II and a high-scoring fighter ace. After the war, he served as the chief of staff of the West German Air Force and as chairman of NATO's Military Committee. He died in 1994.